Crazy House
Copyright © 2010 by Flanagan
Book Design by Tootsie Bellittera

For Britt Strömsted
Whose generosity is unbounded.

Introduction by Paul Quant

Why?

In January 2010, while looking at the Boob Tube I sketched some fat guy. Why?

Years ago when I joined the Navy, the first thing I heard from the guy in charge was, "Ya God damn fuckin Shitheads, line up in a line over there!" There was no simian gesture to where "there" was and the line we were to line up in seemed strange. We were called Shitheads all the time, they got something right, anyone giving himself for "service" must be a kind of Special Shithead.

Consider the profanity, obscenity and scatology of the Navy greeting. My last act of service for my country was to collect the piss bottles of those in bed at the hospital, empty them and return clean bottles to the bedside.

I sublet an apartment in NYC from a dear friend who was in a Veterans Hospital. The building was bought by a Chinaman, and one day five men with notebooks showed up looking at the apartment. A month later, all 10 families in the building got an eviction notice. I was in the Court House at least 18 times (ugly beyond description), my friend dying in the VA Hospital. In the elevator, I heard the two lawyers who were evicting us saying, "he would be dead before they got him out." They were right, he died before eviction. Those two lawyers, fine, fat Jewish boys, never were in the Pacific Theatre to get hurt.

It was in 2001 that I opened my PO Box and found a letter from the IRS, we will take your house, your car, your wages and just about anything left. It was printed in red ink and from two separate IRS offices. They claimed I did not pay my taxes in 1999! It took me about six months to get the bank check print out and you could read many, many numbers and US Treasury and probably IRS. That was not enough, I had to enlarge the back and front so the idiots could see the money was received and cashed, and near the end of this pathetic mess I heard from a judge, advocate or some silly thing saying they would get things right. Right! A month goes by and in the PO box is the same letter, we will take your wages, car, home, children, lungs and kidney if you do not pay your 1999 taxes!

Let me say I always pay my taxes. If I make about $30,000 I pay 42% in taxes, when I made some time ago $80,000 I pay 56% in taxes. Am I half slave and a little free when more than half is taken? That was many years ago but taxes are forever.

My brother who was in the Marines told me to stay away from the VA hospital system. Say about November 2001 I asked to see a doctor. I signed all the papers and was told a letter would be sent for my appointment. After waiting 5 months I called a veterans group and asked about the wait. They laughed and said they were waiting 9 months. 14 months from the time I requested an appointment a letter came. There was no doctor but there was an ugly lady in a white gown who took my blood pressure and said I would get a letter telling me when I could see a PCG (Primary Care Giver). I waited another 4 months and was back in NYC, that is an 18 month wait to see a PCG and if I stayed who knows how long it would have been.

In NYC, a filthy PCG told me to be in at 10 a.m. I waited 'til 2 then to 4 and then to 6:30 p.m. before being called. The lights were being turned off and I got to the pharmacy at 7. That is 9 hours in the God damn filthy gut-busting VA system. I later heard that that lousy pill pusher died and asked how but could not find out, I hoped he died twice from a double cancer. No wonder veterans are suicides today now more than ever.

So this brings me to January 2010 when I go to Social Security for some health care insurance. They tell me I must pay $100 a month as a penalty for lateness. I try to get my application rescinded, and in the effort I write letters indicating that they live in the body of Satan as vampires. I get in the door 4 separate notices to call St. Albans Hospital. I do like a joke, so on April Fools Day I call and am told that in 26 days I can see a "Diagnostic Technician" who will send me to a "Primary Care Giver" who will send me to a "Specialist". I decline. I then get a note from Homeland Security indicating I may be put in jail for 3 years and pay a $10,000 fine, so I call, no answer, call again, no answer, third call, a voice tells me they must send out these letters and that I should frame it, and I should call the next day for the officer on my case. She asks me, do I intend to kill myself, I say no, she asks me if I intend to kill anyone, I answer, no. That is Homeland Security.

So in January 2010 I take up my pen and pencil and being to sketch the dumb buffoons in the Crazy House living of the bile and blood of my experience with the horse shit government. I have sketched and painted most of my life, and as Hung Wong Heavenly Noodle Factory says in a fortune cookie, "A picture is worth a thousand words."

I express myself as all Artists do and I give you my impression of these imbeciles making law and taxing and talking, endless talking to an empty house. I have never voted for fear if I get near a booth I would vomit and swoon into a sickness.

I was like the guy in the movie: "I'm mad as hell and I'm not going to take it anymore!" I have only one prayer, "Please God keep me safe from this God damn fuckin Government."

If you have a morbid curiosity listening to the language of these outstanding gentlemen, sentinels of Democracy, and wish to ennoble your mind with the exotic perfume of their elocution and passionate rapture, be advised, that perpetual verbosity liberally laced with misdirection, bombast and lies, will not stand any exegesis or deep analysis even if expressed with pin stripe suits, red ties and a cheap haircut, it will not cover the empty pomp and fartinacious aggrandizement of these bought lawyers, you will discover with no opacity the rubric of jejune bullshitters.

The basic and intractable problem with the US Government is the coupling of ignorance with arrogance, which is a deadly combination. Ruin is the only result for everyone.

Whenever I listen to Thomas Tallis' great motet, "Spem in Alium," God do not forget me in my lowliness. It brings me to tears. I hope you will find the comedy, cynical humor and the idiots' playground that is before you, amusing.

I spent about 40 to 50 seconds on these fools, anything more would ruin any talent God has bestowed on his lowly servant.

The reader will notice quick notes I made on the sketches which are only for my reference and not meant to be a criticism or comment. With Governor Spitzer I am not sure that $80,000 was the accurate figure for the prostitutes he needed for his sexual activity, it could have been more or a little less, but looking at him and his wife you got to figure more than a dollar was needed to get what he wanted. I can remember guys in the Navy boasting that they never paid for sex, sure if you were a great looking fellow you needed nothing but good looks but Spitzer, wow and that Senator in the toilet or the little boys room, you got to know it's difficult.

I wrote on one General Constipato, well it's known, in the military that in general most Generals are generally constipated and need enemas. They sit at a desk looking at maps and giving orders on the phone, never exercise or have fun and then eating from a can powdered eggs, sausage and bread, no Bourbon or Gin just dirty water ant then no sleep, anyone would be constipated living like that.

I'm sure that is what happened to Petraeus when he swooned, a good enema or at least a walk around the block; by the way did you notice the grotesque ribbons he had to wear ruining the color of the simple uniform, a hideous clash of color and the epilates completely destroying the natural slouch of the shoulders, what a mistake, he could be a very sexy guys if they didn't ruin his appearance with fall da rall.

To go from the ridiculous and the sublime, just look at Charlie Wrangle babed out and he is always babed out, sometimes with white gloves, has about 200 suits and 3,000 ties, this guy knows how to make an appearance, babed out and nice smelling.

Jon Corbino, my first teacher, had a bold, large approach: get a newsprint pad and put it far away from your hand. Work life sized and do not get bogged down with details. Howard Trafton was not an Artist but was very encouraging and urged me to take some liberties and exaggerate certain features. Reginald Marsh had minute poses. When I said I can't do this, he said, yes you can. In a second you can see what is important so you have about a minute to do what you want.

In many scenes in Shakespeare there is the direction: Exit Laughing. I hope this book at least brings a smile.

Media:
1360 Sharpie Fine Point
Pitt Pastel Faber Castel Charcoal
50 Y&C Calligraphy
Pentel
Staple 8.5 x 11 22 lb, Multipurpose white

1

Senator Thompson

A SENATOR

Seth Romeu Burrs

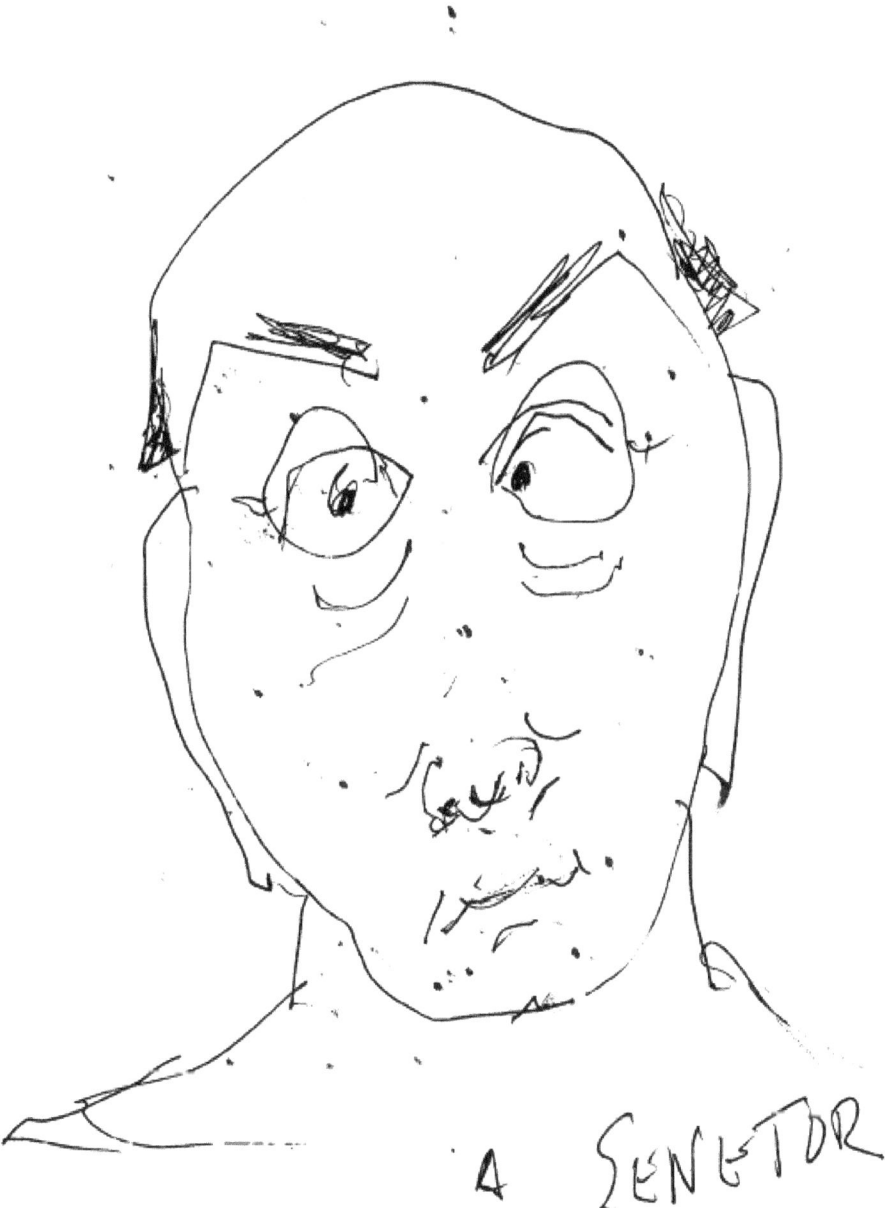
A SENATOR

SATIRE

A work in which vice, follies and stupidities are held up to ridicule.

Gen Billy Ward

11

Gail Rossides — Body Scan Everyone

13

Lsa Jackson
Protecting Enviorm

A DISTINGUISHED SENETOR

CONGRESS

A motley group of gentlemen involved with lies, confusion and obfuscation partially motivated by ignorance, deceit, an irresistible lust for power and fear; uniquely capable of promulgating their authority by taxation and war.

18

19

9-11
CHRISTIE
TODD
WHITMAN

BERTA TITO
DIRTY AIR.

20

Sen. Carl Levin

22

Barny Frank

FOLLIES

Weakness of intellect; a crime; fruitless but expensive undertakings.

(Holy shit, is that prescience, prophecy, prestidigitation, precognition, that is Webster's 1979 Deluxe Edition, is he talking about the U.S. Congress of 2010, give the man the Nostradamus Medal of Fatigue.)

24

HERE COMES WESTERN CIVILIZATION SAVE YOURSELF

I ASK FOR THE AYES AM NAYS

29

30

Mr Royce Freddy 'n Fanny are at fault!!!

33

Louise Slaughter

34

Jack Bohrer
~ I Love ♯♯♯

35

JANDER LEVIN

INTELLIGENCE
Any paper, word or document that some bureaucrat can stamp: "Classified."

36

Pinetta

U.S. CENTRAL COMMAND
ULTIMO
GENERAL
PETR
AUS

39

GOD
BLESS
AMERICA

BRIG GEN JERKY

41

SPENCER
BRONN'S   No SupHOT!!

44

Health Care is Good......

45

9.11
C.T. WHITMAN

CRAZE

To break; make insane; an exaggerated enthusiasm; mania; a fade; fashion

49

50

54

Karen Ignani

Your Health is my concern

Ruth BornBlair
Asst. Regional Director of Inter
Mural and Interfaceing Comittes
For Womans Edjeational Dependencies
For a Democratic America and Co-Chair
of CSD and BFA and SSBD.

LUGAR

JOHN ASHCROFT
G.W. AT. GEN.
LETS GET TOUGH!

POLITICIAN

A select few of the American citizenry gifted with the full knowledge of the fungibility of money and capable of telling special groups what they want to hear.

CRAZY
Unsound; very enthusiastic; eager; wild

Sen. Cardin

Moving forward with the Reconcil. to the Pres. Bill and making available to all Americans and it

1. RISE MR. SPEAKER

British Ambas
to NATO

The Commission has outlined strategic
values concurrent with our security

Rep. Virginia Foxx
 Yield back
Mr. Speaker

99

HOUSE

A shelter where animals are kept; in a zoo, the Monkey House; a place of business, Baudy house, House of Ill fame, Cat House, House of Representatives, Shit House.

100

103

PROTECT
THE US
AGAINST

104

Sen Kyle
The Minority Whip

A GOOD REPUBLICAN

114

Barny Frank

115

A CONCERNED CITIZEN

116

"Timmy" Longman — Senior Research Fellow, VA

THE BUTTERFLY EFFECT
In Palestine, a family that has lived in their house is evicted by some Jews so they can destroy it and make some money in rentals. 4 years, 7 months, 12 days, 10 hours and 35 minutes later, a woman, her two kids and uncle are blown up entering a drug store in Terre Haute, Indiana.

121

1 TRUE MAVERICK

123

A REJECT MAVERICK

124

Maj Gen Lanzn
Dir. of Strtegic Effects
Iraq

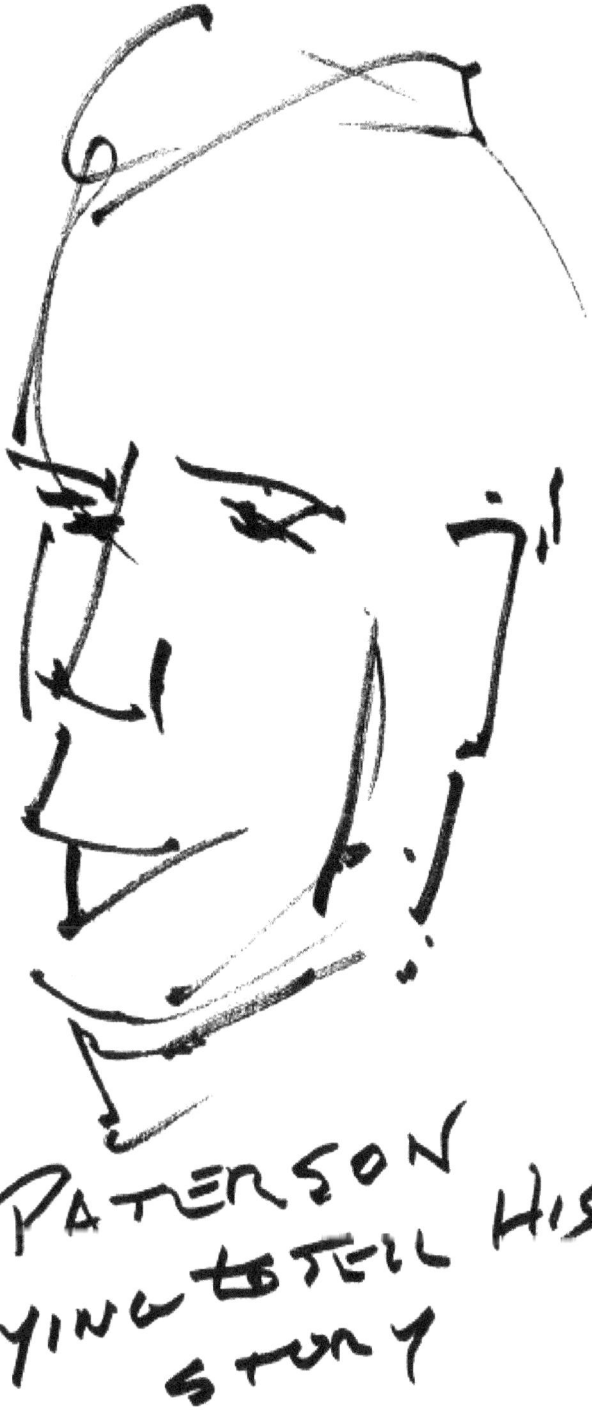

PATERSON
DYING TO TELL HIS
STORY

IVE GOT MINE
SUCKER . . .

129

Rep.
STENY
HOYER
we can move on
if I get out of
the way

130

Rep. Jackson Lee

133

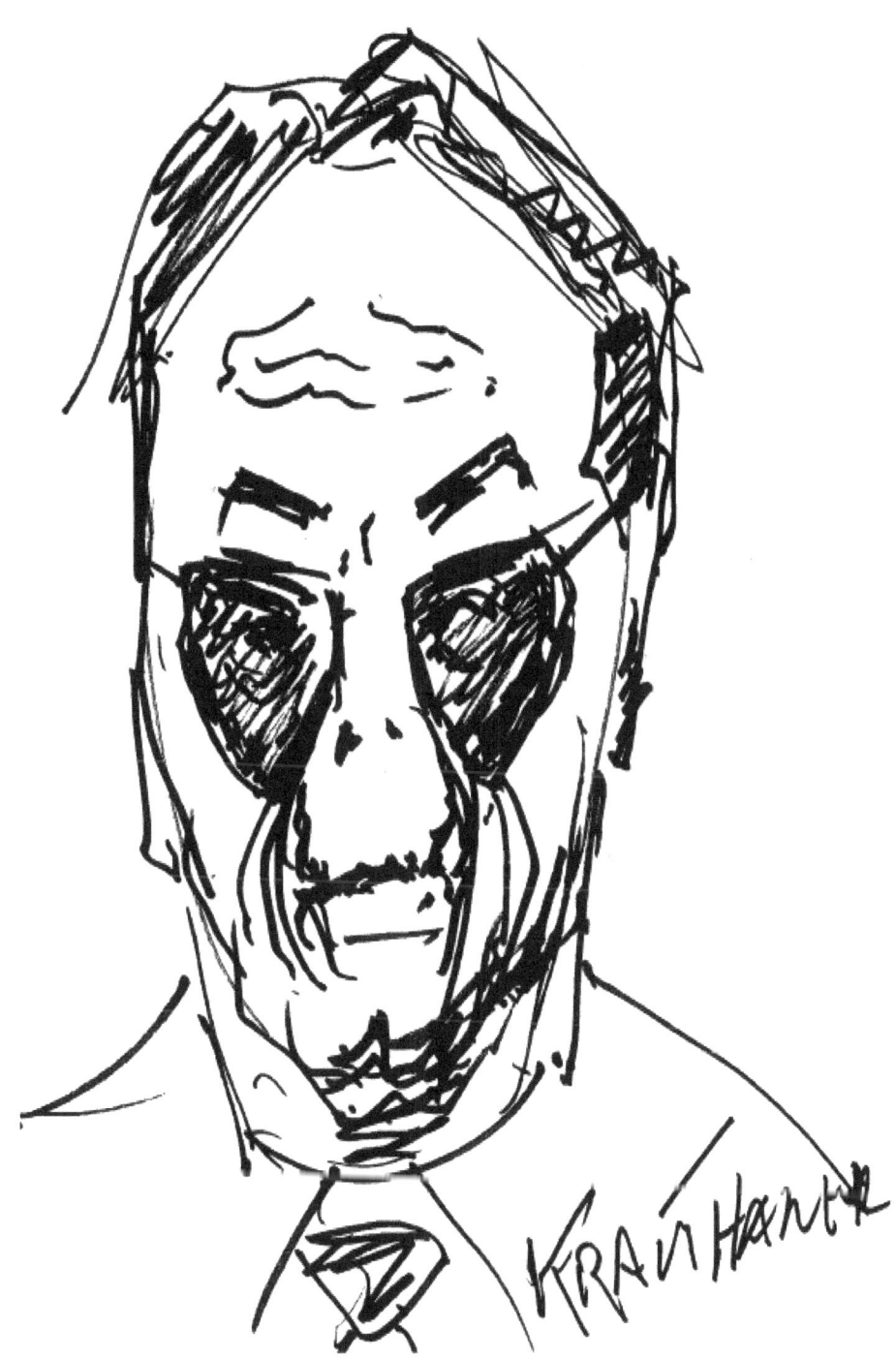

136

TAKE CARE OF THE 800 LB GORILLA: HEALTH CARE

Alice Rivlin

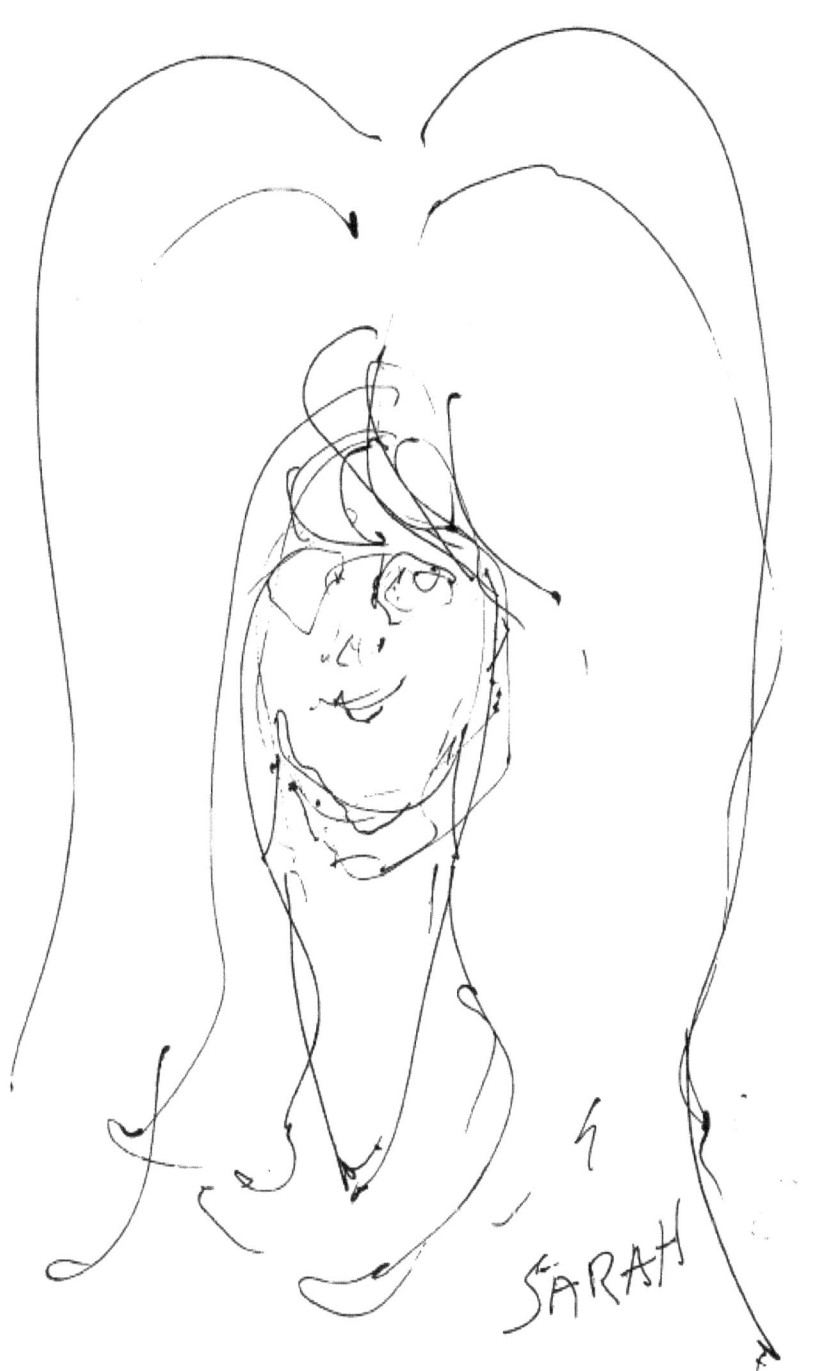

138

A SENATOR

His Greatt
Huliness
Dali Lama

EDUCATE
MEDICATE
INCARCERATE

TEACH EM
DRUG EM
JAIL EM

Gov. of Montana
GOD BLESS AMERICA.

151

UNDESSECRATARY
OF WAR

AN AMERICAN CREED

There is no price too high for the fruits on the tree of Liberty, no road we will not travel to get to that little home on the shiny hill, and there is no sacrifice too great that others may suffer for my safety.

'Ur assessment of the Comitee Report that
the Reconstruction of the BiCameral process—

Profs Roy
Gibson

The Judicial Process has an
ongoing structure which the
President will as it regards so

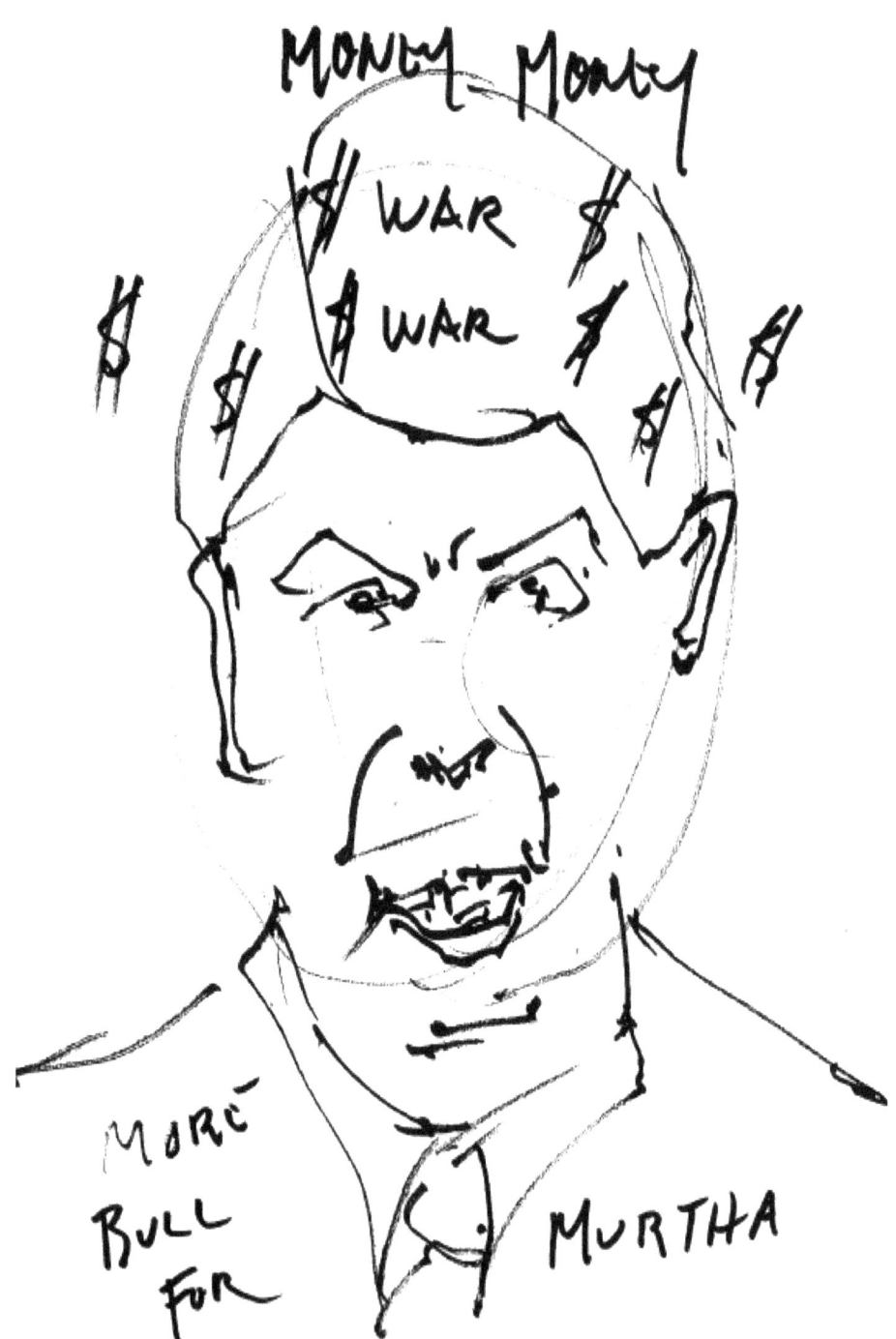

LeMieux Gets Tough with Toyoda

163

166

sotomi year

167

168

171

WE WILL FIX THIS GOD DAMN COUNTRY

SENATOR DODD

174

Spitzer $80,000 for WHOI

VICE

A serious fault of character; grave moral failure; wicked conduct, corruption and depravity.

179

182

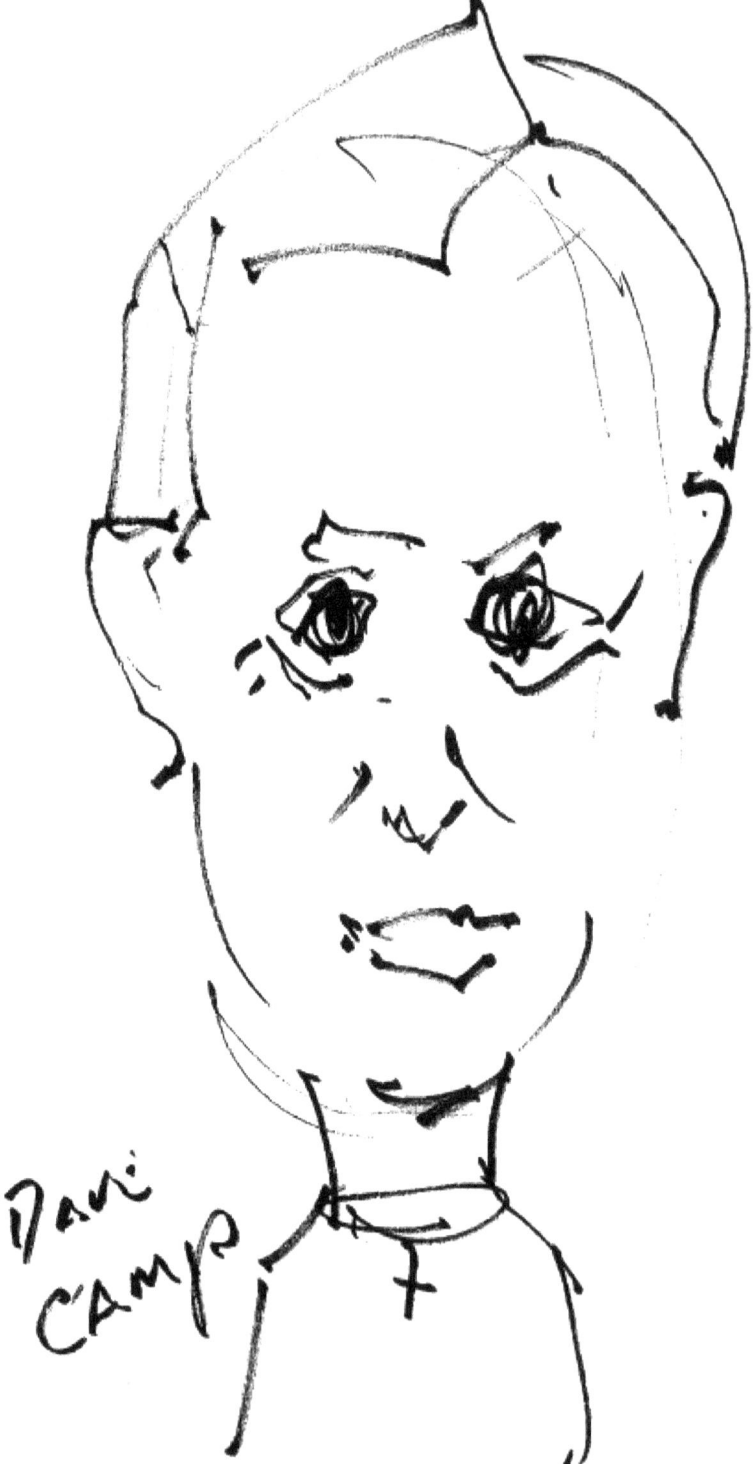

A WANA BE DRIFTING INTO HASBEEN

190

192

Bob
Bishop

193

DEMN PASS
UGH......
JOE BARTON

195

Paul Ryan.

FREEDOM

In the inflationary climate of the USA, the word is so vast, used so often, so common, like "Fuck" it has become a word which has absolutely no meaning at all.

Rep. Boustany

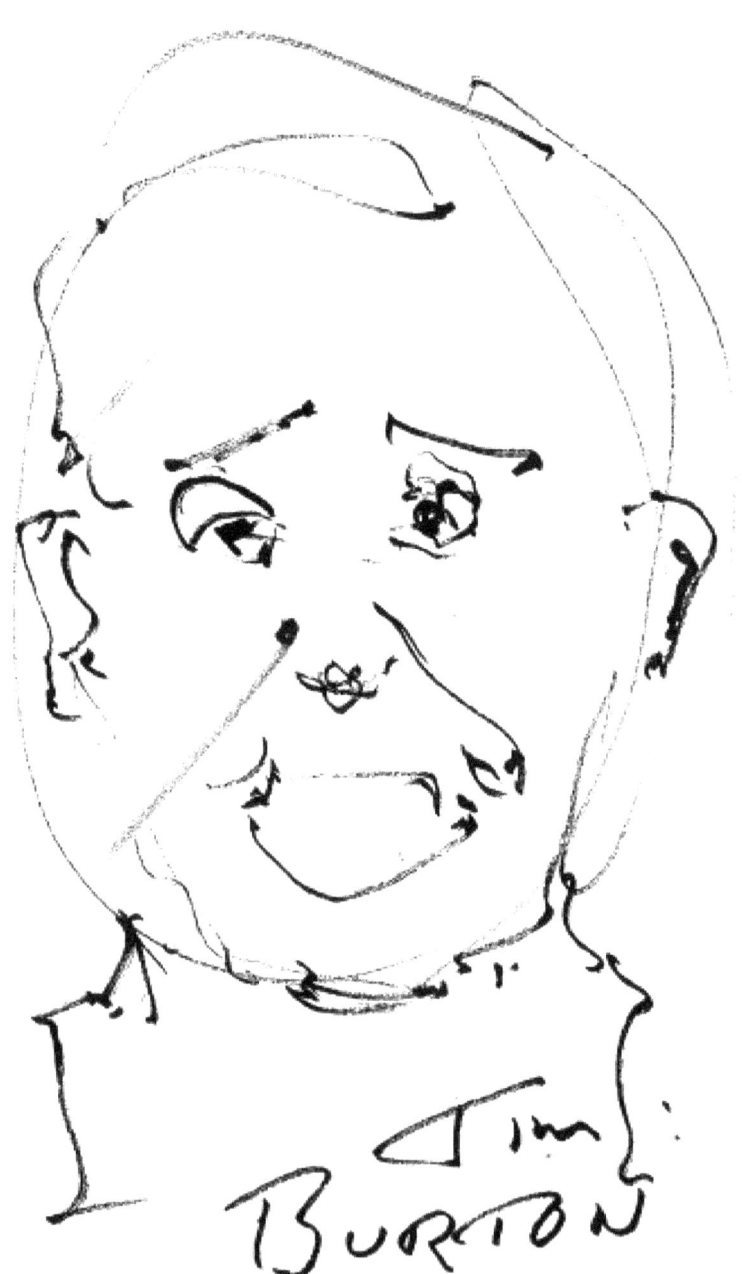

262

TRENT FRANKS

205

Jimmy
OBERSTAR
WE'VE GOT TROUBLE
TROUBLE IN RIVER CITY!!

207

B. KRISTOL

269

$ / A FRIEND OF HEROIC LITTLE ISRAEL $

211

John Boozman

212

I HAVE A
MOTION TO
RECOMMIT

CRAZYWORK
A patchwork making up a crazy quilt.
(Can this be the laws of our nation, the very structure of government?)

WRANGLE IV MILLER

222

226

228

James Klein
Pres. Amer Benefit
Council

231

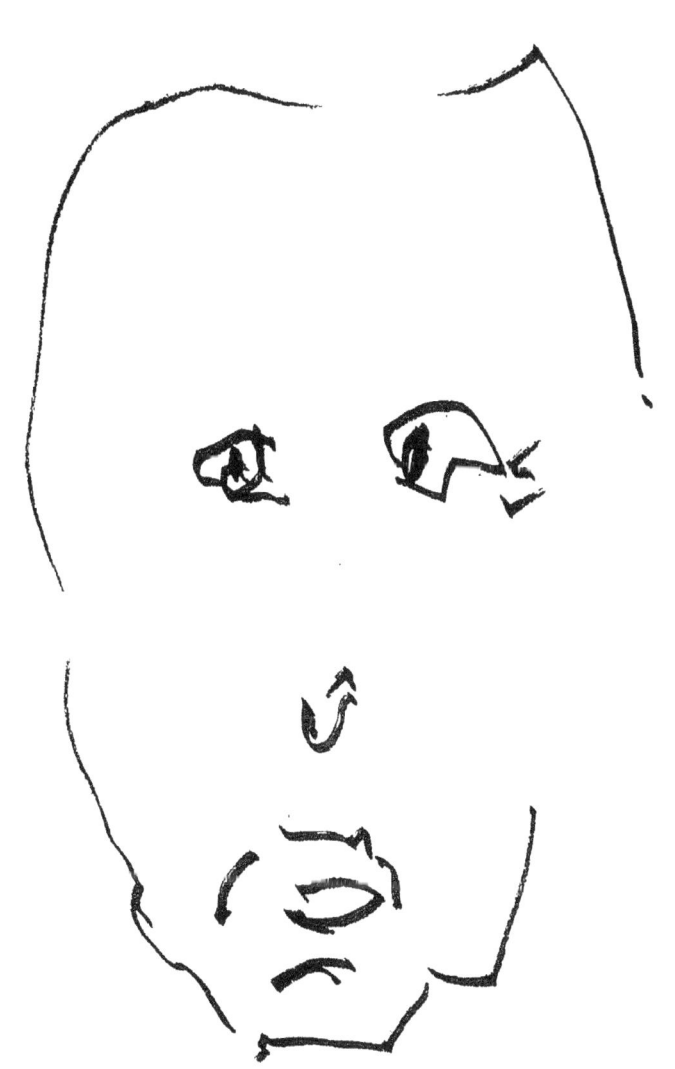

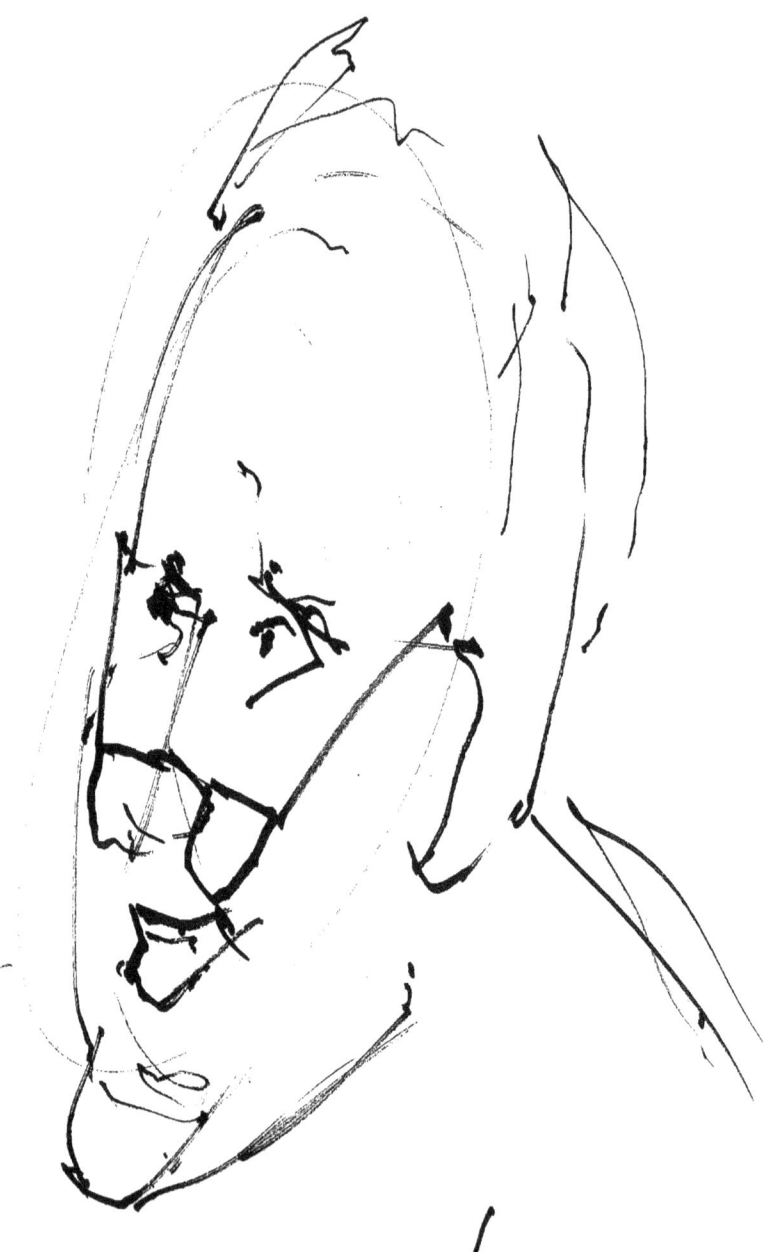

232

Sen. Kaufman

233

Arlen Spector

284

237

PoTuS

238

DEMOCRACY
A word which has such awesome, mega, super power, say in the USA which has never had a Democracy, being a Representative Republic, the mere mention of the word will send thousands out to kill millions.

239

Larry Summers

240

BLANKFIEN

241

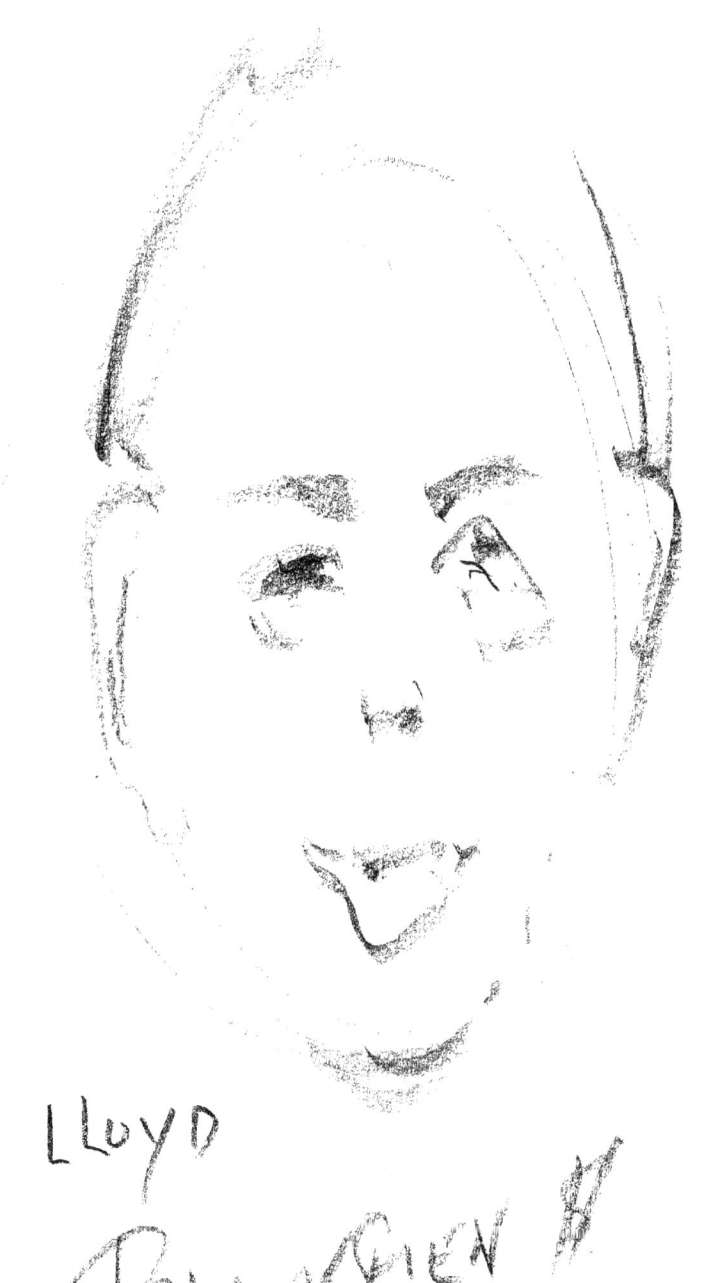
LLoyD
Blankfien

DOCTOR LARRY SUMMERS   I SEE THE FUTURE

246

WAMU
BANK FAILURE
CUT AND PASTE

DAVID SCHNEIDER
REWARD FRAUD
44% MILLIONAIRES

247

248

G.V. AS BLEARY OLD GEEZER

249

256

Rusty Barkery
U.S. Inst of Peace

251

252

John Culberson

Take Back America

258

25g

SHAZMAD

260

Joe Lieberman

General, Sonny I said something to make you swoon

262

SOUTHERN MAVERICK

263

BP
Tony
Hayward

264

Phil Gingrey

265

Bobby Latta

266

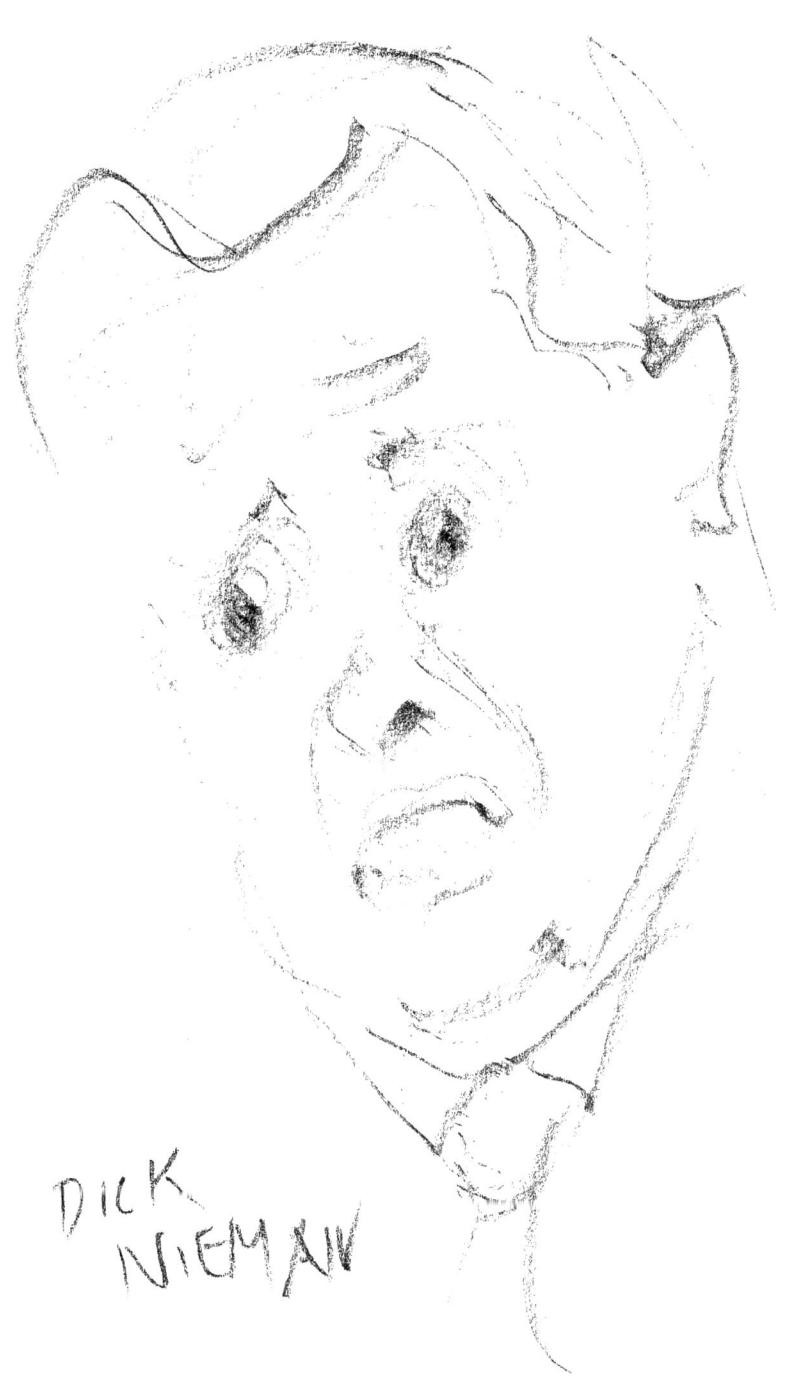

DICK NIEMAN

ISSAC NEWTON
For every action there is a reaction.

267

CHUMMY!
WE MUST MOVE TO
THE DARK SIDE"

268

GENERAL
CONSTIPATO
WE WILL WIN N AFGH

NATIONAL DEFENSE

A modern, very popular notion that we will feel secure in our homes if we make others feel insecure in their home.

Capt. Wood of Prisoner Interogation Famp

Mike Kinsley a wanna be has been

274

Ryan Crocker

275

GENERAL ODIERNO

278

280

GREEN LIZZIE   THERE IS SO MUCH TO BE DONE

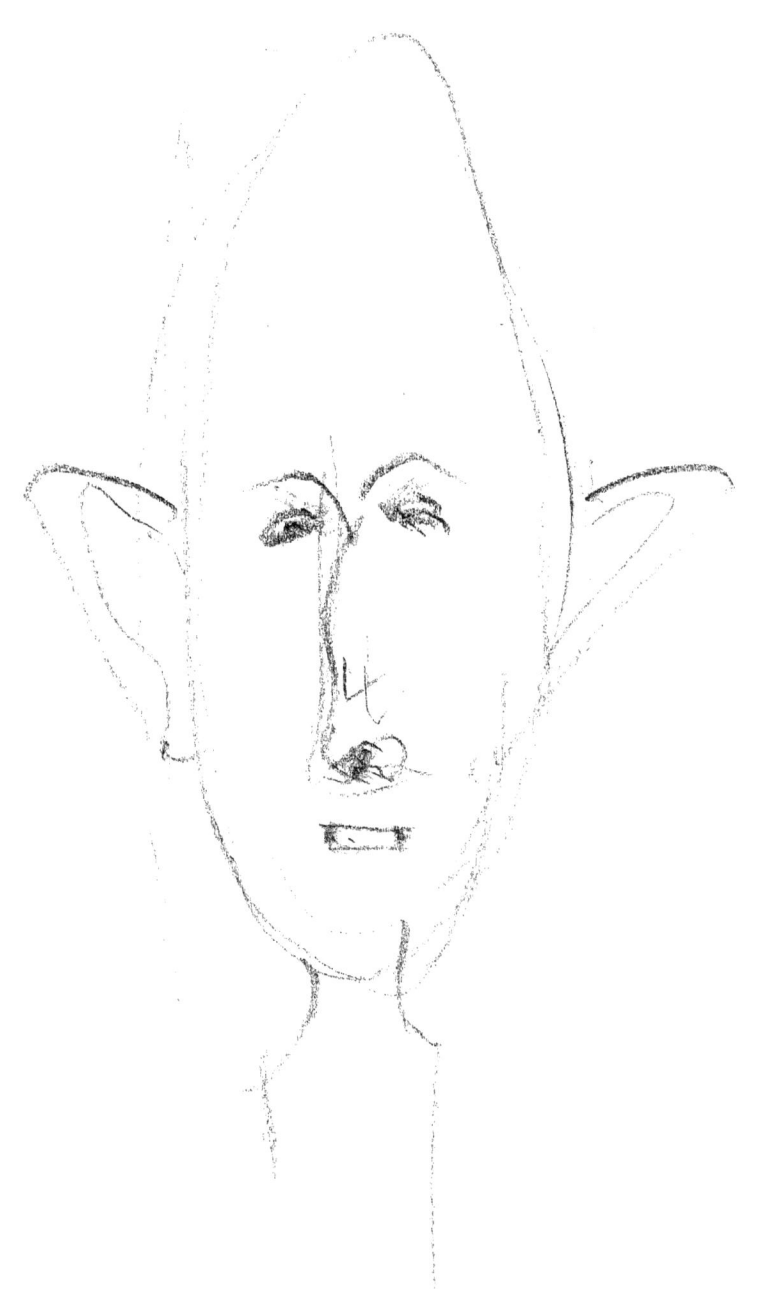

COMMENTARY

These sketches are made from TV, sometimes I could not get the name.

1. A fine example of the bubble head, likes his salary and does what he is told.

2. The jovial simplicity of a child, you to take care of his needs.

3. Anyone appointed by Blagojevich must be interesting.

4. At heart a good man but cannot see the results of any law but enjoys the perks and travel, will wave the flag higher than any televangelist.

5. The high level of debate is amusing.

6. Ah the ladies, thank God, she will not fool with boys in the cloakroom or the kids.

7. There is a feigned honesty in these folks that will disarm you.

8. I love a parade with all our boys and girls led by the best brains in the camp, forge ahead and win one for the Gipper.

9. The military have the look of a cat with the mouse at a desk waiting for coffee, you have not lived before you see a Commander commanding, sometimes there is a hint of worry to see a nuclear weapon explode 2,000 feet over your head.

10. This donkey has studied Descartes, "I think, therefore I am.."

11. Yup, by gumm, jes body scan erverbudy and we uns will be safe, you betcha!

12. This is what I felt like when talking to Social Security.

13. There is nothing like a fat lady to raise your confidence.

14. Thank the Founding Fathers for the courage of Bobby who fought tirelessly for the repeal of "Capital Gains" so America could be

stronger and people could do things with capital. A clarion voice that is missed by every red blooded patriot.

15. This monkey will keep you safe 24 hours a day, God bless America where would we be without him, why we would be bankrupt!

16. Did not get his name, but clearly a man of wit, charm and deep thought. Another champion of man, just give me your money and I will fix it.

17. A distinguished public servant.

18. He is sinking into his own phlegm, I have a portion of his skull open for the gas to escape, Israel as everyone knows is our only salvation.

19. Yup, this babe said the 9/11 air was ok to breathe, golly, why do so many get sick.

20. Levin along with Oberstar and Specter are the great boys for Old Glory, long may she wave, although after the BP testimony the big money said "Eat me" and Carl pretended he did not hear but I hope you know where power is and who makes law.

21. Why, we did not give enough money to the banks?

22. Ya gotta love Barney, I am always reminded of Mr. James Joyce's remark about one he wrote about that whenever he spoke it seemed he was trying to shit from his mouth, Barney they say, is a wonderful guy and is looking after your money.

23. You must see this bozo to believe him, he demands a yes or no answer, he is not pretty.

24. I was thinking of HCE, Here Comes Everyone, grab your shoes, cash and cat, and get the gun over the door, they are out of the cage and coming your way.

25. This nunkwamper thinks he is better than you 'cause he's a minister and can quote Leviticus and Galatians.

26. Had to admire this shit dribbler as he handled the pith and weave of the metaphors he spun like a spider with a mouse, heroic gallantry in the field of words and vote for me.

27. This is what I love about government, at the top in Treasury but did not know how to make out his taxes. Timmy just keeps lookin forward.

28. This guy knows what shell the nut is under, you cannot fool this gem.

29. Talk about greatness, talk about a man who will probe, a man in the shoes of Clay, Calhoun, Kant, this is the face of greatness, behold the Ubermensch.

30. This is not from TV, it is my way of revealing my creative genius, for out of nothing I create a Maverick, the bird in his hair is a gesture to all the little creatures we all love. Rudy ain't the only one who can do Drag.

31. Warning! Watch out for this guy, he can do what the bird of paradise did to the worm.

32. And here I thought it was Jack n Jill, Bourbon n Water, Soup without onions and fake Mavericks.

33. When you couple brains with beauty, watch out, this nation will rise to the top again.

34. Big Jack Boehner, boy can he wear a suit and tie but please Jack, your make-up goes from peach orange to canary yellow and puke green, just settle on cerulean blue mixed with Naples yellow and a touch of Venetian or Terra Rosa, you will be just fine, he has a nice voice too and ladies think he is just fine, could he be POTUS?

35. Like Barney, you gotta love Levin.

36. Talk about pure line, but do not be deceived, this guy is into what you don't want to know about and he looks tied to a sleep whistle, can he get up in time for the big show or will Al Kydee sneak one in on him?

37. Ah, the military mind, give me a bing, give me a bang and a boom, Give me a purge, a surge and a palace behind the lines, give me your poor, your tempest tossed yearning to be free. Freedom and liberty. This is Petraeus, our next POTUS, Yea, he shall scatter the evil doers to the wind, it is said the Anti-Christ was seen in Kiev weeping with his tail limp and leaking stink.

38. I remembered a drawing by George Grosz which shows a sergeant opening the scull of a recruit and scooping his brains out with a spoon and depositing the stuff in a slop bucket. With all the talk about the left side and the right side of the brain box, you go figure, but this is Top Dog War Maker (or Peace Provider), he has the "Grand Strategic Vision", also he accepts the challenge that was given to him to accomplish the mission. Let the politicians argue about what that mission is but let us not argue about the meaning of the word "is".

39. This is a composite, for the greatness of these men cannot fit into a single shoe. It is jerky because I perceived a twitch in his good eye, earned on the field of glory, he sits like a God on a mountain watching over us and he is our salvation.

40. Dare we forget the Hillary part of Billary, the lady who could have been king if only Billy had kept it buttoned up. Did you know she was a lawyer, boy she can take care of things and she stood by her man, let's not forget that.

41. Another mind you can't fool 'cause he is from the South.

42. I don't know anything about most of these monkeys but this fellow I think you better not try to shit on, he is from somewhere and it ain't good to force your welcome.

43. Love these governmentalisticalized minions. ¼ entagonesse is rapturous and intoxicating. How about ultaintermuraliso, islamosistcalized or misunderrepresenalized.

44. One of my best, a happy warrior, can't change a line or dot.

45. Some people are so beautiful that it is nice to do them twice.

46. If I were a mother I would cuddle him to my breast. Oh for the days of Strom Thurmond, the good ole days, the days of wine and roses, Satch Page, the Johnstown flood, a nickel candy bar, a kiss in the dark, nobody did drugs, the Lone Ranger, Peek a Boo, Carl La Fong, capital C small a small r small l, capital L small a, Capital F small o small n small g, Carl La Fong.

47. Another one from memory, our present POTUS, the most powerful man in the history of the world or so they say and they never lie. This is the kind of guy that if he bumped into you would not just keep going but reach down and pick you up and say gee I'm sorry, my fault, are you all right? Or if in a movie show, with one of those endless car chases and police with guns sticking at the end of their arms shot everyone and the theater is almost empty, he sits down next to you and after 2 minutes he puts his hand on your knee and you don't go screaming for the usher but smile and say hi sailor want to have some coffee? And he pays for both. Or running for a cab in this God damn horse shit city he reaches the door handle but says, you take it, and you share the ride which he offers to pay for, that's the kind of guy you have here. He's gonna fix things, you betcha… this fellow is a real Maverick.

48. This amusing chap believed that a trillion dollars were lost, gee where did we lose it, in someone's pocket I think, but just believe it was lost. We just spend money and it gets lost, golly that is what I call careless, as Mr. Wilde would have observed.

49. I like guys who have some papers in hand to wave and talk about cause if you don't have papers you look dumb, and Hank Waxman is no dummy, he heads a committee on government.

50. You know this sterling chap is from the mid or northwest where decent people grow things and vote. You wanna talk about the backbone of a nation, well start talkin.

51. Boy, when I waited 14 months to see a Primary Care Giver in Daytona, then got to see a lady in a white coat to take my blood pressure, then told me to wait for a letter that would say when I could see a Primary Care Giver, and after 4 more months I was back in dirty ole NY, that was some wait for Grimary Care Gifts, this fellow is probably doing a bang up job, fellows of strong will

and know how are at the helm. Tri care is the thing, holistic, top to bottom, inside and out, body and soul, America is at the top. God Bless America! And all those kids over there trying to fool the evil doers.

52. Often I ask myself, is it the big Mafia or just a gang of golfers in pin stripe suits and red ties, are they having as much fun as we are for a lot less money?

53. Being a good American I have learned to love war as it makes you a man. Did you know that according to the Constitution only these bozos in Congress can declare war, thank God 'cause who knows who would be declaring war if not for that little clause in the founding fathers' brain child. I think only one guy has a son in the service against the evil doers, that out of some 250, boy that is patriotism at its worst. If you are not there getting your fuckin legs blown away or some of your brain spilling out you can feel proud when they fold the flag (old glory) and give it to the next of kin, knowing that it is all for Freedom and Democracy.

54. With your health care in the balance, can you doubt a face like this? She is a God sent angel, have no fear for the future, you will be taken care of, if you can find a Primary Health Care Giver.

55. The Second Major Expeditionary Brigade Commander in the Theatre of Armed Conflict, Command Structure, implementing the Projected Force Projection. Larry is here, have no fears. Has anyone ever examined the intricacies of the "Grand Strategic Vision" thing or sought to clarify the admiration of its manifest assumptions, remarkable for its vacuity or the probability of its projective causality? Has any governmental head hunting society published papers, held seminars or issued declarations, albeit presumptuous, regarding the ramifications concomitant to its realization? Is the "Vision" a prophetic utterance reified, an auger, a Divine dispensation granted to a select few? Is the "Strategic" concept a world view of monumental importance? Is it "Grand" because of universal validity, as Entropy or Gravity? In short, is it the veritable, inviolate, sacred word of God spoken only to Dickey and a few friends of equally elevated grandeur? If so, I stand mute. If not: whaddyatalknbout! Better still, if in Brooklyn: Are you kidding me? Or as those with an anemic education, drinking and

smoking cigarettes: You shittin' me?

56. She has looked into the face of war and said, "My Golly!"

57. Behold, Big Dick Cheney, the greatest of all Americans, our Freedom and Democracy are safe and all the world pays homage to this selfless guy who without any personal gain has brought this nation to the apex of dominion.

58. Forget that shit about habeas corpus, torture charges trial, we gonna execute the bastards at that is that, whenever we want to, Washington had Freedom Fighters, they have no uniform, no jats, no Constitution, we are better than the last jerks that were here and you know it.

59. Who gives a fuck for the world, it's America, America it's all there is God Bless America the world needs us we are the most powerful nation in the history of the world, God damn you, kneel and thank us.

60. A life sentence is what he should have, remember Judge Hardy in the movies, probety, honesty, sincerity, good family man, you won't find this guy going into the public urinals for sex or failing to take care of his nephews and brothers in some nice administration's office and if he needs a little yunny here and there, would be hush, hush in the closet. He has his eye on the long term not just the golf ball at his feet. He does have power so if it came to it he could and would destroy you and your family. Just because you don't see him breathing that doesn't mean he is not alive.

61. The work of interfacing committees and program analysis maintaining cash flow with percentage yields concurrent with seasonal percentages relevant to quarterly predictions relating whatever to you know what can be a days work for this minion of our government's salvation, you betcha and don't think that she is so cute you could tempt her sweet hole with candy, ice cream, apple pie or promises of a nice dinner and movie.

62. He looked like 387 but is down to 258, bravo he has NY to help and we need all the help we can get from anyone out there with money.

63. Nothing gets by this fellow, if it were not for the deep South where would we be.

64. If memory serves me it was this sterling chap who headed up Sick Willie's War Dept. and a fine job he did, War Games must have been a lot of fun. Ya gotta figure living under that big capital dome the bad gas must make anyone a little woozy.

65. Another of the fine minions doing the work of the people.

66. It has something to do about the silly guys who want to protect smelt instead of guys like you and me, there ought to be a law.

67. Dingle in a bright moment, they gave him a yes or no, and that is what he wants, Dingle, what a nice name.

68. This man can get tough and gee willekers he is mad as hell with those illegal blokes with no uniform doing us decent people ugly.

69. Poor guy was left by the whore monger Spitzer to take care of all the shit in NY, Spitzer spent only $80,000 for his prostitutes, couldn't he give a million to keep it quiet? Cheap bum, we got Paterson.

70. Could this be Levin again? It don't matter, they are all the same in the backrooms.

71. As a New Yorker I think he should be shown in the best light.

72. His state is bankrupt but he got his.

73. God love him, his Mommy is proud of him, making it in the Capitol.

74. Almost 50% of the Congress are millionaires, ethics problems ain't goin to stop Wrangle from helping his voters to the good life, he is a good dresser too.

75. It's always good for mothers to watch their kids in the playground, you never know who else is watching.

76. It's your money, sucker, that's what we need to do the nice work that we do, keep it coming and you will be surprised with what the future holds for you. I am looking at the small print right now.

77. I bet you didn't know that the Taly Ban, Al Kydee, Asssar bel Awarry, Osama ben Ladid and the War on Poverty, War on Drugs, War on Teenage Pregnant Daughters and the War on Big Oil are not all we have to do, it's the War on Obese Fat Mongers that has seized this monkey, yes sir.

78. Think he is going away this year, he has made enough, good pension, health care (no 18 month wait to see a Primary Health Care Giver) you betcha and he's got friends in high places, hell a lifetime of service has got to get you something.

79. I got Barney with his tongue out, the way you want to remember our Barney.

80. This bozo must dabble in philosophy… "perception"… "reality"… next it will be "the ground of all being" or a world view consistent with money and morality or is existence necessary which has bugged the hell out of me ever since reading Heidegger.

81. The main thing is to keep going forward, don't look back or you might see someone gaining on you, or a poor bastard tripping forward, onward to the shining city on the hill and if you don't get what you want just take it by hook or by crook, it's yours, by golly, and that's what America is all about.

82. I will hazard that this is a loser.

83. Sometimes even the dumbest see the truth if only for a moment.

84. If you want to play in the Crazy House you must play the game, motions, amendments, the yeas n' nays, objections, speeches, motions to recommit, one minute speeches, bla bla bla blablablablablablablab and a lot of other crap that is the way you get things done and move on.

85. One of the greatest Jesusers out there. Just send him your money and get the anointment and blessing that he is selling. If you need it, he will squeeze his eyes and put his hands on the TV and send all good things to you. I heard another Jesuser tell me my parents conceived me in sin and I yelled right back to that idiot that my momma didn't conceive me in sin, you fuckin asshole, she conceived me out of love, jerk weed, go home and pedal

your bullshit to those so ignorant that you're not laughable. Some Jesusers are dopes.

86. Well this jerk is doing it right, object and yield.

87. Unless caught on corruption charges or molesting young boys this joker is set for a long time.

88. Think he is getting out this year, made enough and in other things can make more.

89. This is obviously a man headed for greatness.

90. Another clown moving forward, he is taking all Americans which is nice of him.

91. It's a shame I missed so many names, this man could lead the world if only he had a hat, what little it takes but you used car dealers know that and the doctors n laywers…

92. Don't send everything to heroic little Israel, we need some of it here for the widows and orphans, all the wars we runnin here, let's keep a little for the next war, it's out there, let's go America, movin forward and keep goin, seven come eleven, double down, aces high, gimme a drink, I'm hot and comin out, snake eyes, shit busted again.

93. Why a Brit you ask, well we are everywhere defending Freedom and Democracy, "we bestride the world like a Collossus and…" shit, I swore I would not quote Shakespeare or Milton.

94. Another lady yielding, they do it so nicely, yielding.

95. This lady ain't yielding, she knows her mind and nobody goin to change it.

96. Do you really believe some quirky guy wants to save your money or is he thinking, let me see…. if I…. who can stop me….

97. If he is not proud of Kansas I don't know who is, you know Kansas, what can be said about Kansas, they have hurricanes and let me see…. duh……… ugh……….

98. Don't miss the chance of seeing this babe do her thing, it's worth the price of admission, she is good.

99. They always rise, these people, why?

100. You just got to trust this guy and remember somebody voted for him along with his family.

101. Ted Poe is a very likeable guy, and with Zack Wamp has one of the best names in Congress. I'm sure his family is proud of him, don't' know about Wamp.

102. This could be a plant, they infiltrate everything and you must be on the lookout, he looks dangerous but so do the others. Hope he will be checked out by Security, I don't want to see this guy giving me my medicine or asking questions about my Primary Care Giver, when I get one if ever.

103. Even though they are in Washington and I'm in NY they do frighten me at times when they talk about protecting me against the fellows who are not nice, this fine fellow frightens me so I did not do the best that I could have if he didn't look so, well you know what I mean, I hope. Let me be blunt, if you watch Congress as much as I did you might not sleep too well, I didn't want to have to say that but it's out.

104. It's nice to look forceful and determined in the house of money grubbing and lies, after all the biggest lie is the best lie and if you speak loud enough they will say of you he is a good speaker and if you are around long enough there will be lots n lots of money for you, when you get out to a real job the fact that you look a little odd now will be forgotten. A maker of fortunes, especially your own will go far to move ahead.

105. Here you have the fruits of intellect, a sense of fairness and gol darn apple pie goodness, the Leader, from whom all seek guidance and support, beloved by all even the angels. And she promised to drain the swamp! I'm not telling all I know, it might hurt me I promise to drain the swamp.

106. I think this is what all of us would want to be, noble, true and a good father.

107. A face in the crowd, Democracy at work.

108. Ted is there offering the sagacity that we need in our men.

109. This is one of the inspector guys overseeing the things that need to be looked at, not much gets by him, a real hawk.

110. Think I did Elisha before a rearin back and lettin the lord speak, he knows what a good bullshitter whitey can be.

111. I aim for greatness too, look at the balance, the economy of line, the gesture and geometry, Gad!

112. Miller is a toughy and he will let you know it.

113. Where would this country be if we did not have Republicans to keep us straight.

114. Sometimes I surpass myself without even trying.

115. This is not a self portrait, if I were that good looking I would not have to paint children, they would paint me.

116. This guy has something to do with the VA, this jerk will possibly find a Primary Health Care Giver before 18 months elapse and when I was waiting for a discharge I collected the piss bottles from those without legs or arms and with maybe part of their brain missing, get them enough morphine you fuckin shit bucket feeble bastard, why doesn't someone tell the truth about this craphouse government and stop with the Freedom and Democracy drug and give something to those who cannot live on your God damn fuckin bullshit forever.

117. It's possible he has a porno comic and is saying hmmmm…..

118. That's what we need, drill, baby drill and make America the richest country in the garbage can, yes sir, America the beautiful, I think Americans are the only animals on earth who foul their own nast for a dollar.

119. This is a Bush Baby, it would be illegal to suggest that something be inserted and he would know what it is like for bombs falling on his house. His mustache reminds me of Hitler, did you know the German people loved Hitler, he bathed daily, did not smoke or

drink, loved dogs, was a fine watercolorist which is not easy to do, wanted to build beautiful cities, true to his babe and friends tried to blow the Commies off the planet, he got carried away with the gas ovens but imagine the pressures he suffered, army collapsing, no food, lived in a bunker, probably didn't sleep well, well…..

120. With what he knows, no wonder he looks like this but unless I hear that he is fudge packing some boy in the cloakroom I like this guy, could be wrong as I mostly am, but keep going, Steny, nobody dresses nicer.

121. Just to remind you that the true Maverick is what will save us.

122. Thank God someone is struggling to keep me healthy.

123. Watch out for the reject Maverick, phony to the core, do not listen to his lies, shun his touch, report him to Homeland Security, he is frankly a made over hippie with Mary Jewwanna in his pocket and booze and his breath and a book of his poems in his dirty pockets.

124. Trust this man because he deals with strategic plans to defeat the evil doers and all those who don't know any better. He has his hand on the tiller and is sailing a winning ship. Director of Strategic Effects in Iraq, don't know what it means but it is important for victory. Oh, that grand strategic vision!!

125. Whenever a politician is in trouble they must tell you the true story of the money, the sweetheart or the uncle or trip to Vegas or taxes not paid or the landscaping, decorations and all of the little things we all need to make our life fun.

126. Another look at this adorably sensitive woman who knows how to get things done the old fashioned way, reasonable discourse and head banging, her hair is divine and a glance from her will make your day.

127. We need young, vigorous blood to inflame the spirit of Freedom in us and march ahead boldly into the fat future, rich in lucrative schemes and fabulous wealth.

128. As a weakling you must respect power when you see it, it's really not about country, liberty or even service, it's the cool stance of it's mine and you don't know your ass from your elbow. In this house

of goof balls I take what is here.

129. Steny is talking all the time, talk, talk, talk, but he's lookin good.

130. Thank God we have someone who cares about fashion and she has a good dentist to help keep her good looks, not like the recruits in the Navy where they pull out the front teeth so you look funny.

131. There is nothing like having an expert economic expert giving testimony to the lawmakers, helping to keep this nation in the fine shape that it is in and going strong into the future, yes, going forward.

132. When I was in NYC, the apartment house I lived in with 10 other families was bought by a money bagger in Hong Kong. They had Harriet Fuk of the Fuk Wings get the law firm of Lipschitz, Lipschitz, Goldberg, Silverstein and Shapiro evict everyone. Everyone went but me and after being in court for about a year, the judge said if my rent was raised by 25% I could stay, of course that apt. was in disrepair, so I left. The Lipschitzers were brothers and together they had about 600 lbs. My video, "The Eviction of Jane Doe" was bought by no one. I went to the office of the distinguished Mrs. Mahoney but she was not in. After three visits I was given a card. "Get a lawyer," that was the help I received from the lady. I look upon all who are out of their homes and say, I know what it feels like, brother. Between the Lipschitzers, Miss Fuk and the courts, I gave up., you can fight everything but the stink and the stink will kill you, so go. Yes, go forward.

133. Part of the fourth estate, he sees all between the lines and tells all, probing and with visionary truth lets all of his readers go home happy.

134. Carved in stone by God, National Health Care in this day and age, are you a Commie or just insane, this nonsense must stop before this great nation is ruined. He is not fooled by the abracadabra, hocus pocus dominocus of politicians.

135. Ever ready to assume the responsibility of leadership. This nation must be saved.

136. Oh my heart be still, she was there, she knows what to do, get your note pads out, this beauty can tell the real story. I wonder is she dating anyone now.

137. Sorry Alice, Sarah has captured my heart, what beauty, what a nice dresser and a cute doll, when she is babed out, watch out, she rules. I want her because she is a true Maverick and she is funny, sweet and can see the future. Gee W was funny in the news talks but Sarah is funnier and I want a President who will be funny.

138. Don't know who she is but Drop Dead Gorgeous, enough of the old farts with black suits and red ties, enough I say, don't stop me, DDG is what we need.

139. This is what I mean, tired of watching the uglies but notice the line, the economy, the depth of human compassion the artist shows. He was once a small baby that was loved by a good woman, where did he go wrong?

140. This man could be President if only he was attractive to the ladies, but alas, he ain't hip and probably never was, but he has power and that's what counts, in this nation without that you are nothing.

141. I have come to believe that only the Maverick can save this nation, this fellow looks right if only someone gives him lots of money to get out in the American bull fight.

142. In a world of lies I fell under the spell of deceit, this is not Big Jim, it's some aunt or niece pretending to deal with problems that bedevil this Democracy, she has obviously the intellect and depth of understanding that is needed and could rule with justice or something close to it, probably enjoys a cracker with milk or tea, and won't make trouble when the bombs start falling.

143. I heard he turned down a job in the Oval Office, afraid of pollution and sin, imagine a man in Washington afraid of sin…. never stopped Gee Whizzzickers, our great decider, or any one in Congress, all you need is the natural instinct of greed, a few lies and…..

144. The trouble with a has been is that he is not new and not a Maverick, heavy, sluggish, faded, in a word, a spent force. His day

is over, step aside Newty, it's time for the real Mavericks.

145. Whenever Elijah speaks I listen, a little whimsy, a little whiplash, a little love ya buddy, know what ya feel, remember Sick Willie with his Bible and biting his lip, know your pain, yeah feel your pain, that's what I like to hear. Sometimes you get that only from the big time Jesusers out there, if you send them your money, well Elijah's our hope.

146. You should take a look at the guys who pull the strings on the puppets in Washington.

147. Former drunk and dope addict, now everybody hangs on his every word that comes from his golden throat. Go figure.

148. While doing her shtick before a group of fat feeders, her jokes fell flat, nothing worse than a bad comic is a bad cook. Bill Clinton always makes her sick, why? Please tell us 'cause I wasn't to laugh and it's like Pearl who has that Grand Strategic Vision, let us in on the joke. I bet she wants Bill to take her in his arms and say "you're cute" or "can we have dinner sometime" and I bet she would put on her best shoes. Now Dicky Pearl, his vision even when drunk does not go beyond a dollar bill.

149. The most important thing about a dingo is to keep talking and fool them, that is what is needed and all is well.

150. Educate, Medicate, Incarcerate. Teach em, Drug em, jail the bastards. We need straight talk, no more of this namby pamby bullshit for the gallery. Can we get real. Just get on with the work of America, forget about the details.

151. Another from the fourth estate, the pillar of democracy.

152. You think running a war in four countries and the Tally Ban, Al Kydee and a bunch of other Fierce Fighters is easy or restful, it can make you wonder.

153. This lawyer knows the law and is going to do something when he is ready in a few years and people stop asking questions, after all, the other guy was a bit chancy, at least I know where I am 'cause I got papers.

154. Another distinguished gentleman going to do his business on the floor, his collected speeches will be studied for years.

155. It has something to do with a Bicaneral Report with strings that must be voted out with Yeas and Nays or Up or Down, he gets a nice salary and a man has got to work.

156. Proof positive that you can't cheat an honest man, no, it's never give a sucker a break, no, it's a sucker is born every minute, no, it's members of the jury does this look like a crook, no, it's I have never had sex with that woman. Love his hair, if only I could look like that.

157. Think he spoke at Murtha's funeral. Murtha, who never saw a bullet, gun, missile, bomb or gadget to kill a lot of people that he didn't love, and the people he worked for loved him. It matters not how much you spent, can you put a price on freedom, hell no.

158. It was a grand funeral fit for a king.

159. I must be careful how I speak of this actor on the stage of history for he is our Leader, Savior and Benefactor from whom all good things flow. My genius was unable to capture the prodigious intellect and human compassion embodied in this paragon of nature. Even Rubens would not be able to capture the grandeur of his vision. This pure vessel of all that is nice and tasty like popcorn or a candy bar has given to all of us his mind, body and soul that American may shine brighter on that balloon in the sky.

160. The cozy relationship of the dead heads on TV. Captains of industry and the legislature is ingenious. Play the game of who is the mouthpiece for what or who and where does all that money go.

161. So many clowns live in the armpit of government that you need a score card to follow the game. Across the Heavens wide Champaign, legion upon legion. Swift, rising through the darkness, Light upon Light, intolerable Light bursting the azure… (Forgive my flight upon the mighty wings of Milton, that mighty orb of song, that organ voice, freeing me momentarily from the Stygian sty of these flesh pots, wrangling and rankering for the next dollar bill they can grab, draining the truth out of every verb.) The puissant language of Milton that dashed brute violence with sudden

adoration and blank awe.

162. Get tough with those trying to sell to Americans stuff that is not made in this country. Look at the resolute righteousness of this true blue Public Servant.

163. When you are out of power you must have inspired leadership.

164. Yup you gotta have this guy to make you feel safe and I do most of the time usually.

165. Fat heads rule like pork in the kitchen.

166. It's nice to see a poor girl from the Bronx get ahead, some of them turn to drugs, prostitution, and suicide, or worse.

167. Another example that beauty isn't everything, read books, cook a nice meal and keep your mouth shut goes a long way.

168. I don't' know the name but it is obvious that he is just plain nice, not like some of the others.

169. This fellow has the right name, look at the brains and concentration.

170. My friend Mr. Poe again, just like rhubarb pie in the morning and little yellow flowers. He has it right, don't get angry, you know, "whosoever hates in his heart has already…"

171. Well talk about an angry puss, he needs a drink.

172. Can you believe anyone wanting to impeach our Leader, let the guy do his dirty before we think of impeachment. Give the guy at least seven years, who can tell.

173. Lieberman just don't look right to me, does he sleep too much? Why does he seem to be a piece of dough that was pulled from a nasty place, have you ever seen him laugh?

174. When you spent $80,000 on whores you deserve to be in Congress and he can lie with the best of them, what more do you want, not weird enough? You will wait a long time before something better comes.

175. Here is Hillary who destroys any talent that I pretend to have. She has aged a little ducking those bullets.

176. He looks nice when he smiles.

177. Now you are into real money. About 75% of the budget is in the War Dept. and this able gentleman can control.

178. See what can happen to you if you get near Hillary, I wonder if Big Bill got that way because of Hillary, think about it.

179. Must have been the rackish good looks of this Lothario.

180. Nothing like a happy warrior to give you the guts to swallow the crap that you must. To counter balance the abject misery there must be a jerk who is happy.

181. God! This is what I mean when he smiles.

182. This we ask, where did he come from, who pays him, what has he ever done and why, people voted him in, they chose him.

183. Another question, why?

184. The one minute speeches tell you everything you want.

185. This is big money, the friend of Wall St. who makes it right to do the right thing when wrong thing would be wrong, he does it right for those who are right and not wrong. You might ask what is right or wrong, so you ask Larry and he knows. Right, Wrong, Good, Bad, Saint, Sinner. Criminal, Civil, what's it matter, in the long run God made money so you'd better get yours before it's all gone.

186. When you enter Congress you should try to look honest and don't cry or make funny faces unless you are at a party. It also helps to show intimacy for scripture or something nice.

187. Remember you are not at war, you are defending Freedom or Liberty or Democracy or The Homeland, the Constitution, Our Way of Life, oh yeah, Freedom of Speech, even as Holmes said, yell Fire in a theater, if there is Fire and… well I sent my suggestions for the next Defense of Liberty should be titled "Operation Petals of Peace" or "Flowers of Peace", when you go to slep just say that "Flowers of Peace" but best of all think

"Operation Romantic Interlude", golly that tears me up. I could script the movie with Wanna Srupet as an Israeli freedom fighter and Lance Boffo, an heroic airman shotdown in Bolugistan landing in the middle of a bunch of weapons of mass destruction, and with Wanna they consummate their love on a pile of bombs. Hollywood and Washington must work together for Liberty and of course a little money.

188. We have to keep our spirits up and go forward. It is very important to keep going forward.

189. The last stage of political sefunktery, a wanna be drifting into a has been, not much can be done for him but change political parties or go into charity work where you can make a lot of money.

190. Now we are talking Real Power, not the bullshit variety that the clowns wave around.

191. Step aside for Kevin put a few drinks into this guy and he might say anything. Clean Water, Tax the Rich, Money for Our Boys, Guns for Glory, No Sugar, Flag Day on the Atlantic, Prayer after Meals, Kindergarten Strategic Studies, the North Pole as the 51st State and many other good ideas that will improve the Nation.

192. When you are around thieves and liars you better keep your eyes moving, it might be your money they want or the guy next to you might be masturbating.

193. Sometimes the best of them are confused, the lobbyist didn't explain it, the newspapers have not made it clear, where does a guy turn in this crazy world, Joe is asking himself can the wife help, how about the kids or Tiffany, maybe Hillary can tell him.

194. I love men who think in trillions, boy that gives me confidence that we are going forward.

195. Just look at this rabbit, you better hold on to what you can.

196. You might be deluded enough to think you know who writes the laws or who is operating or judging, this is the guy, you will never see him.

197. I have often thought if you could capture all the bad gas that issues from the speakers in this place you could run a generator in the basement.

198. Whether it's Clyde or Zack or Lyle you can be sure it is your ass he is looking out for and not some gain for himself or being a toady for a multinational.

199. Did Oscar Wilde write "The Fine Art of Lying" or was it Johnson, or was it "The Fine Art of Murder?" Well a lie kills the truth, kill something, be an American.

200. The ultimate master at can do and tell them what they want to hear, a friend of Gee Whizekers and many a rich do gooder.

201. Another clown to stay away from, just move on, let him yell and smile, do not get involved, if they ever take a dislike to you, watch out.

202. Very dangerous, he looks the little boy, it's all surface.

203. He is from CA so don't expect much, which he loves to do.

204. If we had more men like this America would be safe.

205. Being around forever can make you like this, he is going I think, and we will miss his sagacity, wit and just plain Bill way, gosh but he is nice.

206. Think this began as Lundgren but got carried away with his glory, artists are the last people to say they are in control.

207. Billy just keeps on smiling, I bet the next Peace Offensive, you know, "Operation Romantic Interlude" will actually make him laugh, "Operation Oil Rescue" (they got our oil), "Operation Crusade for America," "Operation Final Solution," "Operation Cover My Ass While Running Away." I admit the idea is from Callimachus where one guy says he has to take a leak and the other says wait, which brings the response "why", to which: "we will have something to do while running away." They are of course awaiting armed conflict on the field of glory.

a. I recently heard that a group of Marines were hunkered down somewhere and some of the Afghani "Army" was protecting them, now even some of the dumbest jerk weed Americans have got to say "Huh………"

b. PROTECT. Oh let's sail out a Battleship and, oh get some row boats with fishermen, maybe the Dolphins will PROTECT us… oh….

208. Raw power is wonderful to look upon.

209. This is a friend of heroic little Israel, our only friend in the Mid East. I have heard Israel warns any town 24 hours in advance before bombs are dropped and their hospitals are always open to anyone hurt, now, that's the kind of humane peace offensive we should learn to do, people would like us just as much as they like Israel.

210. You gotta love the weaker sex, oops that's a faux passy, if ever a faux passy was made that's it.

211. Thank God we have a few in Congress who look after us and not just themselves. This is down home goodness, apple pie nice and Beulah Bondi made some cider.

212. Once you master the rules of the place, get back to the Gin game or the babed out babe, be discreet with the babed out babe, it may get you a reprimand or…..

213. The Jesusers on TV say that God can do everything, why does not God take care of heroic little Israel, why do we have to?

214. Wrangle is a wise old guy. Ethics, what the fuck has that got to do with making a dollar?

Excerpts from the screenplay "The Beau Brummel of Kingsbridge Lane" by E. Amanawalla Poot, based on the novel "The Dignified Life of Chamord S W Rinkles," the late, great Senator from Brewster. This historic study was on the best seller list for 24 weeks, the twenty first in a series by the noted novelist Farciot D. Hervearereaeaux.

1.

Fred: Well, he wants to leave with Dignity.

Mable: With what?

Fred: Dignity

Mable: [hammering and flushing is heard in the bathroom, she appears at the door smoking a cigarette] What the hell are you talking about?

Fred: Champs Ringle.

Mable: What's he?

Fred: A Congressman. There is a committee on Ethics, they say he did wrong.

Mable: What does he want?

Fred: Dignity.

Mable: Why?

Fred: He has been in Congress 45 years.

Mable: So?

Fred: They say he might have to go.

Mable: So listen Fred, there is no Ethics Committee in Congress, stop your bullshit and give me a wrench so I can fix this toilet you and your Mick friends have clogged.

2.

Fred: Wankles wants his dignity.

Mable: Wankles, Winkles, Dingle, Dangle, leave me alone.

Fred: He wants his Dignity.

Mable: Who?

Fred: WRINKLES!

Mable: Fred, why the hell are you shouting?

Fred: He's been in Congress 83 years!

Mable: If this Wrankels guy wants his dignity after 83 years I think he should get a job like the rest of us and stop foolin around.

Fred: I think he wants to keep the job he has, he is really a fancy dresser, suave, avuncular, slick, refined, hairy, form fitting, free loader, cane and gloves, rakeish, a bit gassy, flowery cologne, he wears a broad brim hat at the right angle, helluva good dancer and he has a moustache!

Mable: A moustache! Fred what have I told you about the moustache, Tom Dewey, Cronkite, Hitler, and that Bolton guy and Dastardly Dan McGee……. you filthy men, not enough with the hair in your nose and ears but those ugly wrinkled hanging balls you always grab…. Yuck…. Hair everywhere.

Fred: But dear he's 86 years old.

Mable: Eighty six! Jeez he has absolutely no dignity, get rid of the bum.

Fred: Darling, let me make you a drink, we will go to Flanagan's Lounge for a sandwich and a beer, they have the little pretzels that you like, we can watch Hockey on the big screen….. Mable…. Mable dearest don't look at me like that…. I didn't do nothing, it's that Wankle bum…. he's to blame.

3.

Fred: Hey Mable, did you hear that Pelosi wants to drain the swamp?

Mable: Tell Charly to put on his rubbers.

Fred: Rubbers, what do you mean rubbers?

Mable: [appearing at the door, flinging her cigarette butt at Fred's head] What the hell do you think I mean, dummy?

Fred: Well I see by the papers that he wants his dignity and if it is not restored….

Mable: [sitting opposite to Fred] Do you think, darling, tht these clowns sit around all year worrying about their dignity?

Fred: Well you know dignity, pride and fame are important to real men.

Mable: [sipping a bourbon, gin and orange juice drink, her sullen face becoming rigid and her eyes taking on the pallor of a grey wall devoid of intellect, sighs] This is the man I married.

Fred: [did not hear] Rubbers, I don't get it.

Mable: [walks over to Fred, throws the newspaper on the floor] Come to bed I need some relaxation.

Fred But it's only 6 o'clock.

Mable: [she speaks very quietly] Fred……

Fred: [follows Mable, meekly, glancing over his shoulder at the newspaper hawking Wrinkles' dignity] I'll bring a towel dearest.

4.

Fred: Ya know, Mable, some of these Congress people have multiple dwellings, pay no taxes and get a lot of free stuff. For free.

Mable: [appearing at the door of the bathroom, flinging her cigarette butt high in the direction of Fred] What the hell are you jabbering about now?

Fred: It's Winkles, he wants to have dignity, when he goes.

Mable: I thought you said he wants to stay.

Fred: Well he wants to go and he wants to stay.

Mable: Now tell me Fred, do you think there might be something wrong with this Wrinkley guy, he wants dignity going but he is staying, does that seem strange to you?

Fred: He is in Congress.

Mable: [taking a large katorky of Jim Beam with a little ice, settles back and…] My darling spouse, remember that movie with Doug Fairbanks when he gives the officer a gun, to keep his dignity, the music grew softer, the camera on the door, the loud BANG and then they knew he regained his dignity, or in that opera about that little Japanese girl, fucked over by that fuckin God damn Pinkerton shit bag, how she goes behind the curtain and…. Remember how I cried and the music goes all beautiful and loud, she took her dignity and you remember that Jap movie where the old man takes a big sword and puts it into his belly, that was dinity wasn't it……. and that novel where the young man hung himself for dignity……. Come on Fred, don't these donkeys go to the picture shows?

Fred: But Mable

Mable: Shut your mouth about dignity and……

At this point Amanawalla Poot threw a temper rocket and the actors drifted….. Al Wirenstien wanted Liz Taylor and Tony Curtis, they were big in the fifties but Poot insisted in getting Meryl Streep and Pitt but they would not touch this crap, then Poot and Egon Petrovich wanted a Musical with Indian overtones ya know Bangle dangle dancers, wa wa singing and a million extras. Thank God no one considered Dignity.

What has dignity got to do with making a dollar?

Danny DeVito was right, when you die, whoever has the most money, wins. How beautiful Tony Curtis was in the movies, he would love to dance with him, when Marilyn kisses him he should have been there, the kisses of his mouth, his dark hair and eyes, it should have been him. Women with their big bellies, they told me babies come from the gas station, the big pumps, then it was the stork with a diaper, then they said the farm, go get yours from all the rest, how could they tell which one was theirs, and the older boys would tell the dirty truth and it was ugly coming from their big belly in blood and that why did he marry Sophie, she said she loved him married couples happy Al laughed and thought of those big bellies and Tony like a Spring breeze drifted by his mind fragrant dark hair and the dark illuminating soft kisses with Tony could he get him or DeNiro maybe would be Wringles with a moustache, maybe off Broadway but an off Broadway flog would be humiliating, no dignity Poot would get Shirley MacLaine, James Coburn, James Barton, wow double wow what an actor names names drifted over his dollar dream he told Ethel see her strabismus slitting to a lizard look frolic some pow rewind stop action fast forward multiple do dos why did he ever get married when Tony was all he wanted, Al Wirenstein had hope again and dignity and money when he was young would have lots a change in his pocket it made a jingle and when he gave a nickle to some kid they were so happy even kids know it's money this Poot is nice for a flop dad always said be proud you're a good Jew and that is all that matters, never a flop and no one knew of the secret love no one it's about love and money that's a hit and I sent the flowers to Tony withoutmy name on it I didn't want anyone to know people are cruel ruin anyone to get ahead and make money.

5.

Fred: Looky here Honey, in the papers, they gonna clean up America for the comin elections.

Mable: Who's that.

Fred: It's the Teapublicans, they got a contract out on America.

Mable: Well it's about time.

Fred: It says here that all the waste, fraud, corruption, stupidity, lies, whoremongering, theft, pedophiliacs, war mongers, tax evaders, dirty dancers, deferment creeps, embezellers, double dealing, back stabbers, rancourous speechifying loud mouths and others is going to stop.

Mable: Who says?

Fred: Oh it's a guy called Bardy or Army or Blarney. Has got a contract on America.

Mable: [lighting up a second pack while pulling on a vodka] That sounds great.

Fred: Yup, they're going to bring back the Founding Fathers…..

Mable: What about the Mothers?

Fred: Oh sure, the Founding Fathers and the Founding Mothers who made America decent, good and nice.

Mable: Who is doing this wonderous thing?

Fred: The Teapublicans, Blarny and Gingrich, he was a teacher and….

Mable: He got fat, seen him on TV.

Fred: Yeah, but there is a lot of them to get America moving in the right direction and make us proud again.

Mable: What they goin' to do with all the evil doers?

Fred: Didn't read about that yet.

Mable: [finishing her drink, goes back to the bathroom with a wrench and hammer] Fix some cocktails, Fred.

Fred: [reads on, wide eyed, feelin good] Boy these guys are goin to make America safe for Americans! Shall I stir, not shake?

Mable: That's my honeybunch.

Fred: [he was humbled and exhalted at the thought of our Founding Fathers, Washington and Jefferson, who knew the value of a horse, donkey, cow or Negro slave. When you could get some cocaine, to ease the pain, at the corner drug store without big Pharma or the greedy doctors interfering and you had a gun to keep your family safe. Women knew their place in the kitchen. No wrinkled up Social Security minions to lie to you. "Stay out of forging/forcing entanglements" meant what it said. Fred like brave Cortez, dashed on a peak in Darian gazed in wild surprise above the newspaper headlines and looked into this wonderful world of Americanism and political Dogoodyness. With misty eyes he gasped….] Gee Willikers!

215. This is not Kip Bond, I think it was my genius trying to catch that moment when the thing turns into Dorian Grey., I heard "stay the course", that must have triggered by Muse, it happened before in 56 and 206. After $3,000,000,000,000 and many parts of our boys and girls leaving parts in the sand, and the thought of yellow cake, WMD and a mushroom cloud, mission accomplished, evil doers, Freedom, Liberty, well you know the slogans. Kip is so amiable so dang Freudish, so charming like in old Vienna, you would like to have him meet your sister and Aunt Jenny for some cookies and tea. Cookies and Ovaltine. Cookies and Coco. Cookies and Ice Cream.

216. I have a few notions of the ideal Congressman, this is one of them.

217. Two of the nicest boys in the bunch.

218. Doing his best to do something good for America.

219. The greatest Jurist on the Supreme Court, our Constitution is the Bible and he is the reaser of mysteries and solver of puzzles and looks very sexy in black.

220. Chucky is a real actor, has a sense for the camera angle and will talk about anything, will protect heroic little Israel with the last drop of our blood, the tree of liberty must be nourished with the blood of patriots now and then, but I think he cannot go further, he is not a Maverick.

221. Clearly this man is made for greatness.

222. Praise the Lord, there are a few who are harmless, I hope.

223. I will not do a faux passy on this lovely gem.

224. Shit, greatness deserves an encore.

225. Save America Paul, you can do it, I know you can.

226. You know that oil spill down in the Gulf, you know the problem, we got to help these fellows clean it and it might take some $$$$$$$$$ but we got to do it, they did the best for the Company but we got to get doing what America does best…. Moving forward…

227. The only good mayor NYC ever had was LaGuardia, all the rest are bums, but Koch, why doesn't he just go away, why does he put his 2 ½ cents in whenever some dead head asks him "what do you think"? Just go to Florida.

228. Part of the vast number for minions that pull down this creaky old country. Who needs him.

229. Let me count the Peace Efforts here and there, Iraq, Afghanistan, Pakistan, maybe some proves into Lebanon, trouble in Korea, some pirates out there and Iran is, don't think they just make jokes for the newsies and have a drink, they call him the Veep.

230. Too bad you can't put this morbid mole under glass and preserve him for study, his contribution to his Nation is… wow… a sketch cannot capture this toad.

231. After Greenspan this is all I could do.

232. Him and Levin should get glasses that fit.

233. Would you believe he dropped the Republicans to get elected by the Democrats, but they said, drop dead you old fuck, the magic bullet that went sideways up and down and then goes into someone near JFK, holy shit that is some bullet. End game, an old geezer who should geezer himself out.

234. I imagined Gee Whizakers, at sometime was a kid, pulling wings off of butterflies and saying to Daddy, I wanna be a big shot some day.

235. The Holy Trinity, Geithner, Rubin, Summers and with Paulson and Greenspan we had the best of all possible worlds. Golly someone up there likes us. God Bless America, we are the greatest Nation in the history of the world, and all with Gee Whizakers for 8 years, how did we get so lucky, I ask you.

236. Just another glimpse of the beloved Larry, no it's Alan, how could I make such a mistake.

237. This is the Great Decider after he was told the difference between the Dodgers and the Yankees or Night and Day, he said, "Huh?" and asked for his pretzels and popcorn. They say the insane are

very happy, if they don't like the clothes they must wear, will throw them away and they masturbate whenever they like, after all what is the difference between them and us, it's really about which side of the fence you're on.

238. This is Gee Whizekers at a later time when he did not get his sardine, cucumber and peanut butter sandwich, "Arrgh!"

239. After doing Bush twice I was discombobulated and this fartinacious joke did not help.

240. What is it that the handling of money does this to you?

241. When you deal in Crap, Junk and Shit you will begin to look like Crap, Junk and Shit, even with makeup on. It all seems to show in the face, you remember Dorian Gray.

242. Is it true that when Nero was dying he said, "I want to help someone," he gasped, "Who can I help?" Some clown stepped forward, Nero pulled him down to his deathbed and whispered in his ear, "Help me."

243. The job is beginning to show.

244. If you traded $100,000,000,000.00 a day this is what it would do for you. Now that is not just dollars, it could be empty air or something that clever people invent, or it could be just plain regular, run of the mill, crap. Shit and not of the highest grade. Suppose you had a hole and you sold it to someone and that guy made 20 pieces of the hole and sold part of it to someone else, not telling him it is a piece of the hole, and then…. well… let it go if you want to sleep at night. Dick can explain it better 'cause he is smarter than me.

245. We have men that can see the future and it is Good. It is nice.

246. No worry for you, these Rabbits know what they are doing and, they know, don't worry. They will take care of things, do not worry. They will move ahead. Forward.

247. Is this handsome man worried, trust him and pay your taxes, support the kids over there and hang out your flag.

248. As Gee Whiz approaches Geezerhood and thinks back on life, he made no mistakes, we know that, but did he get what he wanted? You might think he wanted some oil fields, maybe a football team or just a beer with Coca-Cola and chicken liver, tomato, avocado with catsup on whole wheat and a few olives, but I think he would like a trip on the merry go round without daddy watching him so he would say, "See" and as he grows into that age where wisdom blooms and the vanity of life is laughable, someone would read to him the books he never read, and when he was put into his bed he would say, "Gee" and go to sleep.

249. I thought I would give you a fright. Yes, this is Alan.

250. Who would have thunk that amidst the glory of war we have an Institute for Peace? They count the number of bombs and missiles aiming them toward the peace places and marines ready to fight for peace anywhere in the world. You can sign up for peace and no one will call you a "Peacenik," today you are a "Peace Provider for World Renewal and Agape."

251. This is the Dick we all got to believe in 'cause he did what had to be done and no one can say it violated the Spirit of America, always remember he had knowledge no one else had, so who can say, he is not the kind of man that would lie. You know it's said Dick hunts quail, Jesus, nobody hunts a little bird, you might track, stalk, shoot but not hunt. Some people hunt lions, tigers or wild boar with angry horns turn on you, some bastardos have hunted elephants, but quail? Imagine the little creatures turning on Dick, oh what a fright! He unloads the double barrel at a few feet, what's left of the poor little thing. I wonder if he wears those blubberbutton clothes with the Sherlock Holmes cap.

252. That thing in the Gulf, it just blowed up, go figure, the darn thing just blowed up.

253. The Prez. Of BP, it just blowed up, that's what it did, blowed up.

254. Yup it just blowed up, we will take care of the oil, can you believe it, that damn thing just blowed up. We'll move forward now.

255. He will defend heroic little Israel and he will get anyone who tries to shit on America so watch out this fellow is tough and he don't fool.

256. Just so you know a real Maverick, make no mistakes with the fakers or pretenders.

257. Another example to watch out for, we need men like this to save us and give the security that we need.

258. This was not taken from TV, he is just too large for TV. Behold the Ideal Senator Dortmund Epper, part time Minister, considers Catholics idolaters, Jews unclean, Negroes subhuman and Americanism must be taught in our schools. Raises his four daughters in strict Leviticus law. Enjoys being in the gym where young men sweat and bathe. Reads the local newspaper for intellectual stimulation, wears the same black suit he graduated in. Epper will listen to you but is only interested in the core beliefs he knows to be true. Will consider a bid for the highest office of leadership. Has a small copy of the Constitution in his pocket. Considered by some to be stern but they have never been to the movies with him laughing at Bob Hope and Jerry Lewis although when it became known that Jerry was a Jew didn't laugh much anymore. Is in constant contact with the well known Jesusers, a Tay-ak-son, when speaking only in spiritual tongues, "gaallouiqwuillangogrkrltpxbutjgdfmjjmjponrigalogfj." And so on.

259. Can you imagine Shahzad almost destroyed NYC with bombs made from the super market. Do you remember Gee Whiz told us to fight them over there so we would not have to fight them here, come on America, let's pull together and forward, that's it, forward, that shining city on the hill, we have a dream, forward, let's move forward.

260. Bless this man for bringing forth that babed out Sarah. I pray she will be the funny POTUS we all want, although see 281 regarding my worries. This sketch was made five seconds before Gen. Petraeus swooned at the table under the blistering questions of Lieberman, wow, they wanted to hear what was said to POTUS, the poor General swooned but when he came back the kow tow began, it was special.

261. Lieberman made us proud in his apology, which was almost as good as the "Apology for My Life" which I have been writing for the past 33 years.

262. The South has the best Mavericks but California is coming on, moving forward.

263. If you had ruined a major coastal area with the fish and wildlife you would look like this, but drill baby drill.

264. Think I saw this clown before.

265. Toxic assets and infinite balance sheets with corporate bonds, derivatives and stuff like that, he has his eye on it all, you betcha, you're not going to put anything over on this fellow, the big time Capitalists are watching this bozo, you can bet on that.

266. Dick might just be having a bad memory or he might know something we don't or it could be personal, ya know what was called the shock of recognition.

267. This is the Dick we love and admire, moving to the dark side, well at least he likes it. I must admit it made me just a tad sick, but I don't count. He made a lot of money for a few people, God Bless Him and God Bless America and all of the boys and girls bringing Peace and Freedom to everybody. Do you remember the movie with Karloff as the monster, when seeing some light says…… Graah…. Grrah…. And he waves his arms wildly…… Grrraaaahhhh……

268. There is no substitute for Victory.

269. Ah, the glories of Gitmo and the fight to get to the truth. Pulpification is when you beat or pound the body many times so the bones and other stuff become a mash that renders use in the future impossible. I think our doctors are working on the pulpification of the torso and making the arms and legs operate or pulpifying the head and having a gizmo stuck in the neck that can steer the buggy.. I am not sure if Miller invented pulpification or if someone in the CIA or FBI told him how to pulpify a prisoner.

    pulp. noun.
    A soft formless mass that sticks together.

Pulpification. Noun.
The act of converting into pulp.

When prisoners were beaten for weeks, the arm or leg would be pulpified and there would be no major organ failure (the stated definition of torture). The arm or arms or the leg or legs would have to be cut off. If the removal of arms or legs was not done the prisoner would die. The reason would have to be decided by the doctor in charge. Such is the raise of the meager minds mufticating on the Grand Strategic Vision which is the American foundation for the moral parameters of Civilization.

270. She knew how to interrogate prisoners, you betcha!

271. You can tell the intellect of Tesla or Gauss is here. Can't he just go away... do we need a Jerry Lewis comeback...... is Liz Taylor fat…….. did Joe Penner finally sell his duck.

272. Thank God we have somebody making war on that oil gusher a mile down, I just hope it's better than the War on Poverty.

273. Just because he looks mentally sick that does not mean he is. This Patriot has the world at his fingertips.

Don't ever make the mistake of thinking Negroponte is mentally ill, because you could disappear very quick, this man is the most powerful man in Washington. Feared by everyone. He heads more Bureaus, Committees, Departments, any office could be his. FBI (Fuckin Bastard Imbecile) CIA (Completely Insane Apes) SSS (Senile Seniors Society) and so many more that I can give only a partial listing of the vast offices of this man, can you imagine the weight on this man's shoulders and the decisions that must be made? Few men could undertake his mission for Freedom, Democracy, Security, Capitalism and old fashioned American decency.

This man might be in control of 15 offices that keep the security of this great nation inviolate. The budget may be greater than $100,000,000,000.00!

I will suggest a few more:

EET (Emerging Energy Technologies)
CHT (Committee on Homeland Terrorists)
FRM (Federal Rape Management)
ARS (American Rapists Society)
HOL (Hedge fund Open-ended Larceny)
UOO (Undersecretary Overseeing Options)
PHQ (Primary Health Quality)
ANN (Amalgamated National Negotiators)
PRK (Politically Responsive Know-it-alls)
BUBL (Bureau Undersecretary Before Legislation)
SUC (Socially Undesirable Committee)
ERS (Essential Response Services)

274. This guy surprises himself by the action he takes.

275. This great leader of the awesome might of this great Nation with bombs, bullets, men and an Army, Air Force, Navy and those quirky Mariners, wow, what a force, what power, what leadership. This is the man who knows how to do it, watch out all of you fellows out there who think that just because we lost in… well, forget that stuff, let's move ahead, let's go forward. There is victory if we stay the course, let's get behind our boys and girls. Remember Nixon and his victory fingers, what a splendid gesture!

276. Billy is beginning to take on that paunchy, saited look so common to those in the Crazy House that I hope he avoids the pitfalls in Washington and does not fall into the stink hole of some whore and have to apologize, or worse, be found touching the testicles of an under aged boy, perish the thought.

277. I love to hear them talk about Moral Hazard….. Ground of all Being…. Necessary Existence…. Categorical Imperative… Enhanced Interrogation… Money in the Bank… Cocktail Parties… Slush Funds… Lobbyists… Lies… War.

278. A day does not go by without this charmer putting in her two cents.

279. Ecce Homo. If you are to look upon greatness. Sit down Daniel Webster, be silent Henry Clay, Calhoun, Lincoln and William Jennings Bryant. This nation will not be nailed upon a cross of

gold, never, for this man has in his vest pocket book and that book is the Constitution.

280. This book which has begun in the white heat of passion, as just about everything an Artist will do, had to end somewhere but I did not know until I saw Queen Lizzy and her hat, even I had to sit back and wonder, that hat! Who is she? In this day of celebrity and PR did someone choose that hat for this occasion or was it chance? I watched for a very short time and then moved on, ya know, movin on, movin forward and that stuff, I did the sketch and said this is it.

281. In the few moments while doing Queeny I thought of the one to follow her, the Prince, and could see Dana Carvey and his rendition of this fine fellow which was as a little speech he would make about being a tampon in the trousers of his loved one and the things he would do. This made me think of a sketch which I discarded but did not throw away and it was that ketch of someone I could not remember would be the perfect finale. It was the Tampon American in all his glory, there must be someone who elects these dumb balls to Congress, this must be him, Mr. Tampon America. Now consider this, the Congress has dedicated this year as the year of the woman, so my sketch of Dortmund Epper the great Senator from Ta yak sus has to give place for the coming woman.

Lynn Thordyke as I remember said in the last stages of the decay of Empire, the homosexual and the female will come to the fore. So here we are.

That cute babe, all babed out with her baby talk, Sarah, will not make it, damn I want a President who will be funny, guess it will be a Lesbian who is a mixture of Maxine Waters, Hillary, 9/11 Whitman and Sotomayor….. ugh….. Mr. Americus Tamponi.

TEILHARD DE CHARDIN

The crucifixion is perpetual.

www.ingramcontent.com/pod-product-compliance
Lightning Source LLC
Chambersburg PA
CBHW070553100426
42744CB00006B/265